THE PROMS

Also by Leslie Ayre:

THE WIT OF MUSIC

THE PROMS

by Leslie Ayre

With a Foreword by
Sir Adrian Boult

LESLIE FREWIN : LONDON

To Janet

First published 1968
by Leslie Frewin Publishers Limited
15 Hay's Mews, Berkeley Square, London, W1

This book is set in Baskerville
Printed by Anchor Press
and bound by William Brendon
both of Tiptree, Essex

09 089010 8

CONTENTS

Introduction
by Sir Adrian Boult

I T IS A great privilege and honour to write this short introduction for Mr Ayre's history of the Henry Wood Promenade Concerts.

It goes without saying that they are a wonderful institution. I like to think of the deep impression that a visit to one of these wonderful concerts makes on any foreigner, or indeed Britisher, who has not seen that audience before. It always seems that the average age is getting younger and younger. That is obviously not so, but it is a continual refreshment to come and see the expression on the faces of people who stand to listen to the music, sometimes for hours on end.

As a performer, it is always a thrill to take part in any of these concerts, and I know my colleagues, thinking particularly of the late Sir Malcolm Sargent and Mr Basil Cameron, and all the soloists, are particularly happy to take part in Sir Henry Wood's great foundation and to look up to his figure in bronze, which presides from the organ gallery and looks so benevolently down upon us all.

I am sure the book will be eagerly read by thousands of Promenaders, and I wish it every success.

1

OVERTURE

IN THE CROWD jostling out of the Royal Albert Hall
after a promenade concert, a pretty teenager was
heard to say to her boy-friend: 'Where *was* Queen's
Hall anyway?'

What a question to ask! *Where was Queen's Hall?*
Why, the child must be mad! She might just as well
have asked whose face that is that looks out towards the
audience from behind the orchestra on every night of
the Proms.

But, of course, impatience gives way to the realisation
that, though she may be a devoted Prommer of today,
the questioning teenager was not even born when
Queen's Hall became overnight no more than a
memory, a cherished memory, to thousands upon
thousands of music-lovers. And, since they were first
launched upon Victorian London, the Proms themselves have changed as much as have the clothes and
the skirt-lengths of the eager crowd in the promenade.

It had to be so. The Proms have always been
changing, either through deliberate act of will or
through force of circumstance, sometimes force of
circumstance of the most violent sort. There have been
times when it has seemed that they would have to
vanish from the national scene because of pressures
financial or arguments airborne. They have survived

the hard facts of finance and the blast of Hitler's bombs and they are young and healthy. Though born away back in 1895, they still have the ebullient enthusiasm of youth – in their devoted audiences and in the great number of young artists to whom, as has always been their way, the Proms hold out a welcoming hand at the threshold of their careers. Each season they present a proportion of works new to our ears – and some of them surely do more violence to those ears than did the 'novelties' of years ago to the ears of the early Prommers. Or do they? Those early Prommers were not faced by Boulez or Stockhausen but they did have the somewhat shaking experience of encountering the likes of Schoenberg and Bartók for the first time.

True, the intimacy and the sense of 'dropping in among friends', which was such an endearing characteristic of Queen's Hall, has given place to music in the wide open spaces of the Royal Albert Hall. But, strangely, though indicative of the unique place won by the Proms in the hearts of music-lovers through the years, something of that feeling of friendly informality and of sharing in the evening's music-making has been carried over. The sense of rapport between audience and artists, fostered from the earliest days, is one of the notable survivals from the splendid past.

The Proms certainly have changed. For years, the weight of each season was carried by one orchestra and one truly extraordinary man, Henry J Wood, whose contribution to the raising of orchestral standards and the development of public knowledge, appreciation, and love of music was greater than that of any other single individual in the history of this country.

In the last season for which details are available there were fourteen orchestras, thirty conductors (some of them conducting only one of their own compositions), twenty-four choirs, eighty-three vocal soloists (twenty-eight of them making Prom débuts), and sixty-six instrumental soloists (thirty of them making débuts) – a massive jigsaw puzzle for the planners.

But as our teenager was in questioning mood, we might reasonably ask in our turn: 'Where are the Prommers anyway?'

Pedantically, we go to the dictionary and confirm that, when one promenades, one 'takes a leisurely walk, generally in a public place, for amusement, exercise or to show oneself off'. Whereas it is true that, on the famous 'Last Nights', many are to be seen harmlessly and usually amusingly showing themselves off, there is little evidence of leisurely strolling around or of conversing with one's friends if the music should be on the dull side – or, perhaps, of chatting even more animatedly if the musical background should take a gay turn.

But the great numbers of people who have fallen in love with these series of concerts have not been of the pedantic sort. They have made their way to Queen's Hall or the Royal Albert Hall to discover, enjoy, and be refreshed by music. Promenade concerts they certainly were in their origins and the title, The Proms, with all its nostalgic overtones, properly persists to describe what has now become the biggest music festival in the world. There may be no promenading, but The Proms they will always be.

Who, then, are the Prommers? There is a tendency to think of them as only those who gather in the arena, stoically standing up throughout the concert – though occasionally requiring the attention of the ambulance people – and, on the 'Last Night', donning their most comical get-ups, waving their umbrellas and their banners with the strange devices, and greeting favourite players by their first names. Yet there are many who, perforce or by choice, sit out the evening and who would insist that they, too, are Prommers, with the same youthfulness of spirit that buoyed them up when they used to stand for hours in the promenade of Queen's Hall, and that it is only the powers of endurance of their feet and perhaps the increased importance they have placed upon comfort that have changed. Once a Prommer, always a Prommer – even if the old pins are not what they were!

They all add up together into the most extra-ordinary audience in the world, an audience whose concentration and abounding enthusiasm stagger and delight the many foreign artists who appear in the Proms of today.

That very enthusiasm has brought down upon the heads of Prom audiences the snooty criticism that they will cheer anything indiscriminately and that they really have not the remotest idea of what it is all about.

It is an easy jibe and one that is not new. It was heard in Sir Henry Wood's day – and he vigorously opposed any such view. After all, he more than any-body else knew that, as a result of the Proms and, later, of the advent of the radio and the gramophone, 'popular' audiences were becoming steadily more knowledgeable and discerning. He set out from the start to encourage the love of music. Not for him was the narrow-minded attitude and the contention that only certain in-the-know folk can get joy out of music. He applied himself quite deliberately to the task of bringing music to the ordinary chap and showing him what it had to offer, in the certain belief that experience and familiarity would bring in their wake knowledge and some sense of taste. One suspects that Sir Henry, conscious of this criticism of his enthusiastic Prom audiences, was not in the least put out by the reception accorded to Schoenberg's *Five Orchestral Pieces* when he gave them their first performance in this country. The audience hissed heartily. Far from being annoyed, Sir Henry, one would imagine, took it as a legitimate expression of opinion, giving the lie to the accusation of indiscriminate enthusiastic acceptance of whatever came along. And time has shown how far-seeing he was – as on so many other occasions – in including the Schoenberg pieces in his programme. Few could have realised at that time that the day would come when a Prom audience would almost bring the house down with their cheers after a full concert performance of Schoenberg's *Moses and Aaron* by Covent Garden Opera.

Infectious enthusiasm there undoubtedly is at the Proms, and this atmosphere of sheer enjoyment of music has not come about by accident. The sense of oneness between audience and performers was deliberately encouraged and built up from the start. Henry Wood made a point of introducing his principal orchestral players – several of whom were also heard as soloists – to his audience, thus creating almost a 'family' atmosphere of making music together. That was, of course, in the days of one orchestra and one conductor throughout the season, but the policy was

13

so solidly and understandingly founded that its effects have remained through the years. When Wood said that he wished that all concerts were as 'Bohemian' as the Proms – and he conducted great numbers of other important concerts – he was surely referring to the all-friends-together atmosphere in the enjoyment of music. It was all part of the process of cultivating a devoted audience for the promenade concerts.

But let us assume that some of the youngest of the Prommers really do not know much of what the music is about – if indeed music is *about* anything – and that they are there mainly because Promming is the done thing in their particular circle of friends. Does it matter very much? The important thing is that they are there – and there are many worse places for young people to be – and many of them will continue to be there for season after season, experiencing an extraordinary range of music and forming their own tastes and standards. After all, quite a lot of the older and now more experienced members of the audiences of today must have started in just that way.

Many of the young ones, of course, are there not just because it is the done thing, but because they *want to know*, and because they realise that the way to get to know about music is not just to read books about it but to listen to lots of it. And it is fascinating, by the way, to observe how often the younger element in the audience, their minds uncluttered by fixed ideas and prejudices, take with obvious enjoyment to works which, to older ears, are decidedly 'difficult', even forbidding.

In the London of the eighteen-nineties, concerts of

14

good quality music and of a decent standard of performance were limited almost entirely to the comparatively narrow circles of well-to-do concert-goers who had their own favourite series. There was hardly anything at all for the 'ordinary' intelligent person – and there were many who were only too ready to be encouraged. There was, of course, no radio and the main musical diet was the drawing-room ballad, all very well in its way but decidedly limited in scope. Uncle George singing a rollicking bass song to Auntie Ethel's tentative piano accompaniment might have been all right, but there was more to music than that.

The Queen's Hall Proms were cunningly devised to lead on from the drawing-room ballads and the light-weight waltzes to the richer fare of great orchestral music, and they admirably met the need with an educational process that was not only painless but positively joyous. They had the breath of youth in them from the start and they broke down the barriers of musical snobbery. Their torchbearer, Henry Wood, was only twenty-six years old and the whole enterprise tingled with the spirit of enterprise and adventurous purpose.

Since those days, the radio and the gramophone record have exercised enormous influence on the musical tastes of 'ordinary' people, but it was the Proms which made the first great breakthrough with their practical message that music is for the many and not just for the privileged few. There never has been a time when the general listening public was better informed than it is today.

There is indeed point to the story of the horn-player

15

who, carrying his oddly-shaped instrument-case, climbed on to a bus bound for the Royal Albert Hall.

'What have you got there, guv?' inquired the conductor.

'It is a French horn', replied the musician, coldly, as he paid his fare.

'What are they playing at the Albert 'All tonight?' pursued the conductor.

'We are performing the Fourth Symphony of Beethoven', was the reply, in a tone calculated to discourage further aimless conversation.

In due course the bus reached the Albert Hall and the passengers clambered out.

'Goodnight, guv', called out the conductor. 'Don't forget to watch that top E Flat in the slow movement'.

So much for 'ordinary' people knowing nothing about it.

2

PROMS — EARLY STYLE

WE MUST LEAVE that somewhat subdued horn-player hurrying through the artists' entrance of the Royal Albert Hall, and take a look at how it all started.

Even two hundred years ago it was possible to attend promenade concerts in London; but these were of an alfresco sort and it was not until a good many years later that anything really comparable with our idea of Proms came upon the scene. But one of the remarkable features about the endurance of the Proms and their seemingly limitless future is that, when they were founded in 1895, it was not a new idea to present series of concerts at which a section of the audience stood or strolled around instead of sitting in seats. Indeed, Robert Newman himself – Robert Newman whose idea it was to launch the Queen's Hall Proms – had had an early brief experience of this kind of thing at Covent Garden.

One of the earliest forms of 'promenading' to music was to be found in the pleasure-gardens of the London of the eighteenth and nineteenth centuries – Vauxhall Gardens in Lambeth, Marylebone Gardens, and Ranelagh Gardens, on the site of what is now the Royal Hospital, Chelsea.

Vauxhall Gardens were opened in 1732 and an orchestra was installed as early as 1758. They were

B

closed down in 1859, to the accompaniment of a fire-work display ending with an elaborate setpiece, 'Farewell for Ever'. Marylebone Gardens flourished up to 1777. Ranelagh Gardens opened in 1742 and carried on until 1804. The end of these diversions was to a considerable extent due to the activities of rowdy elements whose idea of an entertaining evening embraced anything but music.

Charles Dickens gives a racy account of a visit to Vauxhall Gardens:

> A small party of dismal men in cocked hats were executing the overture to *Tancredi*, and a numerous assemblage of ladies and gentlemen, with their families, had rushed from the half-emptied stout mugs in the supper-boxes, and crowded to the spot. Intense was the low murmur of admiration when a particu-larly small gentleman, in a dress-coat, led on a particularly tall lady in a blue sarsenet pelisse and bonnet of the same, ornamented with large white feathers, and forthwith commenced a plaintive duet . . ..

> It was a beautiful duet: first the small gentleman asked a question, and then the tall lady answered it; then the small gentleman and the tall lady sang together most melodiously; then the small gentleman went through a little piece of vehemence by himself, and got very tenor indeed, in the excitement of his feelings, to which the lady responded in a similar manner; then the small gentleman had a shake or two, after which the tall lady did the same, and then they both merged imperceptibly into the original air; and the band wound themselves up to a pitch of fury, and the small gentleman handed the tall lady out, and the applause was rapturous.

For those who found the musical entertainment less

than enchanting there were rope-dancing and a balloon ascent nearby. Dickens does not seem to have encountered one of the more exalted forms of promenade concert – but it is significant to find the idea of throwing in additional forms of attraction, an idea that was to persist even into the early days of our own Proms.

But these were open-air affairs in the London gardens, as distinct from concerts presented in a hall in which space for promenading has been specifically provided.

The earliest equivalents of the promenade concerts as we think of them were presented in Paris in 1833 by Philippe Musard, and five years later similar entertainments were put on at the English Opera House – concerts *à la Musard* they were called – and the charge for admission was one shilling. The audience were able to stroll around or take a drink while the orchestra dispensed a programme usually consisting of four overtures, four quadrilles, four waltzes, and an instrumental solo – and the solo on the wind instrument was to be a popular feature of our own early Proms. Soon afterwards, Musard himself came to London.

The English Opera House had already had a varied career. It was opened on the site of the present Lyceum Theatre and was originally intended as a showplace for the Society of Arts. But the Society did not last long and, after various vicissitudes – Madame Tussaud's waxworks were presented there at one time – the building was licensed as a theatre. In 1831 its name was changed to the English Opera House.

Promenade concerts quickly became a popular form of entertainment in London—though the background of popping champagne corks would not seem to have been particularly helpful to discerning listeners. Indeed, the tendency seems to have been to regard the *music* as a pleasant background to amiable conversation and the convivial glass.

Similar entertainments were put on at the Crown and Anchor Tavern, in the Strand, and, in 1840, Proms – *Concerts d'Été* – were presented at Drury Lane by the English violinist Eliason, with the assistance of a remarkable Frenchman called Louis Antoine Jullien, then only twenty-eight. No expense was spared in making a show of these affairs and the music was played by an orchestra of about a hundred.

It was not long before Jullien became a leading light in the Drury Lane concerts, which he carried on with the title *Concerts d'Hiver*. His avowed purpose was to popularise music and he would go to any lengths in the way of showmanship in order to achieve that end. His ambition knew few limits. He went bankrupt at least twice and he finished up in an asylum in Paris at the age of forty-eight. Hardly an encouraging augury of the hazards of promoting promenade concerts.

Despite his flamboyant antics, Jullien was not by any means a mere charlatan posturing before his audiences and dispensing musical trivialities. Born in Paris in 1812, he soon became a competent musician and composed and conducted a good deal of dance music when still a very young man. But he was broke by the time he was twenty-six and it was then that he departed from Paris to try his luck in London.

At one stage he was giving nightly concerts in the Surrey Gardens with an orchestra of three hundred, offering programmes of waltzes and quadrilles, but

also sometimes including symphonies or single movements from them. He believed in doing things in a big
way and was sometimes known to bring in six extra
brass bands!

From Drury Lane he moved on to give series of
concerts at Covent Garden, making a special feature
of his 'Monster Quadrilles', composed for particular
occasions. He was at pains to present himself in
accordance with the popular idea of what a musician
should look like. His hair was long and wild and he
conducted with frenzied gestures which provided
entertainment even for the least musically interested
members of his audiences.

His most ambitious items were carefully stage-
managed so as to achieve the maximum dramatic
effect. Behind him would be placed a chair, upholstered
in velvet. In the full fire of the climax of the piece he
would snatch an instrument from one of the members
of the orchestra and throw himself into the general
uproar. And at the end he would fall back in a state
of collapse into his strategically placed chair. His
audiences could hardly complain that he did not give
histrionic value for money.

But for Beethoven he had a particularly impressive
ritual. Before starting the work he would ostentatiously
draw on a pair of white kid gloves, and a minion would
bring him a jewelled baton on a silver salver. It has
to be said for him, however, that he did give his
popular London audiences a taste of the music of
Beethoven. Rossini's *Stabat Mater*, too, was among the
works performed by him for the first time in England.

Jullien was an admirer of Berlioz, about whom he
wrote a book, and one of his ambitious ventures was

to invite the composer over to England. The plan was that Berlioz would get ten thousand francs as conductor, another ten thousand francs would be set aside as expenses of the concerts, and there would be a commission for Berlioz to write a full-length opera for the second season. But the whole enterprise proved to be a fiasco and Berlioz went back to Paris—without his money.

Jullien himself wrote an opera, *Pietro il Grande*, presented at his own expense at Covent Garden but bitterly condemned as 'the most deplorable event of the season – a specimen of vulgar pretension that was most deservedly hissed off the stage'. It was withdrawn after five performances and cost him thousands of pounds. He tried his luck in America and, back in London again, lost more money in the Royal Surrey Gardens Company. After a farewell concert at the English Opera House and a tour of the provinces he returned to Paris, there to be arrested for debt and imprisoned. He was released, but only to await his end.

A strange and tragic career, indeed; but a kindly thought may be spared for Jullien as at least an ambitious entertainer who tried to bring music to the people and who, as such, was one of the pioneers of promenade concerts in this country.

After Jullien's time at Covent Garden, the concerts there were conducted by a number of different men, among them Alfred Mellon, Jules Rivière, Arthur Sullivan, Joseph Barnby, Luigi Arditi, Alfred Cellier, Frederic Cowen, and Crowe, the programme content varying from the serious to vocal waltzes, sung by girls in fancy dress, with such words as :

See-saw, See-Saw,
  Here we go up and down.
See-saw, See-saw,
  All the way to London Town.

Early promenade concerts also included those given
by Balfe at Her Majesty's Theatre, and a series at the
Royal Adelaide Galleries, Lowther Arcade, where the
additional attractions included 'dissolving views' and
'The Laughing Gas every Tuesday and Saturday
evening', whatever that may have been.

One of the dominant features of music in this
country in the last century was the oratorio, poured
out in such numbers and of such variable quality as
to have been referred to as the 'oratorio industry'.
There was, of course, merit in some of these works,
but many of them were turgid affairs with little
imagination about them.

It would not be true to say that, in the time
immediately before the launching of the Queen's Hall
Proms in 1895, London was without music. But in the
main it was for rather specialised sections of the public;
there was little for the ordinary music-lover or for
those, who given encouragement, might be induced
to take an interest. The short series of Hans Richter
concerts at St James's Hall, and those of the Philharmonic Society attracted their particular publics and
there were the concerts of the Royal Choral Society
at the Royal Albert Hall as well as Monday and
Saturday concerts of chamber music. Georg Henschel,
with his London Symphony Concerts, made an effort
to popularise good music but did not win great support.
Most significant of all in this respect were the Saturday

23

afternoon concerts conducted from 1855 until 1901 by August (later Sir August) Manns, who did extremely important work in developing the musical taste of the public. But there was nothing of quite that nature in central London.

Yet there were signs that there was an untapped public. The time was ripe for a full-scale effort by the right men in the right place. The place arose with the building of Queen's Hall – and the men were ready to seize their opportunity.

3

RIGHT PLACE — RIGHT MEN

INSTEAD OF A much-loved concert hall, there might have been a skating rink on the site just north of Oxford Circus, right in the heart of London. That was one of the plans put forward but, fortunately for the story of London's musical development, it fell through before it got very far.

In Langham Place, hard by All Souls' Church, with its candle-snuffer spire, built by Nash earlier in the last century, the site on which Queen's Hall was to stand was occupied by the Portland Bazaar and some livery stables and dwelling-houses. Leases on the property had been acquired by the Crown who, in 1887, entered into an agreement with F W Mackenzie Ravenscroft whereby a concert hall was to be built on the site – and a splendid site it was for a concert hall.

Building operations began in 1891 to the designs of two architects, T E Knightley and C J Phipps, and the hall was completed two years later. The interior was elaborately ornamented, though the predominant colouring of the walls was, on the insistence of Knightley, a somewhat off-putting grey.

Knightley seems to have made a special point of this matter of colouring, for, as Robert Elkin has recorded in *Queen's Hall, 1893–1941*, he picked as his pattern the particular shade of the belly of a London mouse. In order that his wishes might be meticulously carried out, he went so far as to keep a string of dead mice in the paint-shop as models of what he desired – a decidedly macabre approach to the creation of what was to be the home of beautiful music. Warm strawberry-coloured furnishings did, however, provide cheering contrast to the predominant greyness.

In the building of later concert halls in this country and elsewhere, great play has been made of the science of acoustics, with elaborate tests involving the firing of pistols and other means of assessing resonances. By whatever means they brought it about, the architects of Queen's Hall certainly knew their business, for whenever the talk of musicians of today goes back nostalgically to the old place there is invariably reference to the excellence of the acoustics of the place.

In the original scheme there was a Royal Box in the centre of the grand circle but this was soon removed. The interesting circumstances of its removal are described by Ivor Newton in *At the Piano – Ivor Newton*[1]:

> The first event there, I was told by Armine Bevan, one of its original directors, was a smoking concert given by the Royal Amateur Orchestral Society, with Queen Victoria's son, the Duke of Edinburgh, as leader, and the Prince of Wales (afterwards King Edward VII) as its guest of honour. A table in front of the stalls held cigars and opera hats. During the course of the evening my friend, as he was to become, was presented to the Prince.
>
> 'This is a lovely hall', said His Royal Highness. 'I like it. But' – pointing to an ornate structure in the middle of the circle – 'what is the purpose of that odd-looking enclosure?'

[1] *At the Piano – Ivor Newton*, Ivor Newton, Hamish Hamilton.

'That is the Royal Box, sir', replied Bevan.

The Prince studied it more carefully for a moment, and then laughed. 'You'll never see me in there', he said.

The Royal Box was removed that day, and the hall existed without any special accommodation for royalty until its destruction in the last war.

Even so, King George V and Queen Mary did attend a Prom at Queen's Hall in 1924.

The first lessee and manager of Queen's Hall was Robert Newman, then aged thirty-five, who was that unusual combination of the lover of the arts and the tough, astute and imaginative business man. Indeed, his life up to that time had embraced both music and business.

Newman loved music from his early days, but in fact began his career by spending a year or two in business in the City of London before deciding to go off to Italy to study singing. He sang professionally as a bass for six years, sang at a Prom at Her Majesty's Theatre, and was chosen by Parry to sing the title part in his oratorio, *Job*. After a spell as concert agent, he entered the Royal Academy of Music, where one of his fellow-students was a young man called Henry J Wood, eleven years younger than himself.

After brief experience at Covent Garden, where promenade concerts were being presented, Newman went to Queen's Hall and his first function there was a children's party, followed in the evening by the concert of the Royal Amateur Orchestral Society. The programme was a mixed affair; and it is interesting to note that it contained Mendelssohn's *Ruy Blas* overture, which was to be the last work performed at a Prom

27

before Queen's Hall was destroyed by German bombers many years later.

Frederic Cowen, with whom Newman had been associated at Covent Garden, conducted the 'official' opening concert, a performance of Mendelssohn's *Hymn of Praise*. In the next two years there were various series of concerts with distinguished artists, among them being the conductor Siegfried Wagner, son of the composer. Newman was an ardent Wagnerian enthusiast.

It seems likely, however, that, right from the time he took over Queen's Hall, Newman was thinking of launching series of promenade concerts. He did not rush into it, but laid his plans carefully. With his prominent moustache, he looked rather like Lord Kitchener in his younger days and somewhat like Elgar later in life, and, though he had a decidedly kindly streak in his nature, he was a blunt business man who knew what he wanted and was determined to get it. What he wanted to do was to raise the standard of popular musical taste in London, and he intended to do it by recruiting a young, energetic and imaginative conductor, not necessarily a particularly well-known man, but one who, through his talents and personality, would attract and cultivate a loyal concert-going public. If he was also a keen Wagner enthusiast and a potentially distinguished Wagner conductor, all the better.

At this time there came into the picture Dr George Clark Cathcart, one of London's leading ear, nose and throat specialists, with consulting rooms in Upper Wimpole Street. In the course of a casual encounter, he heard from Wood that Newman was considering a scheme for presenting promenade concerts in Queen's Hall. With certain reservations, Cathcart was enthusiastic about the plan and asked to be introduced to Newman.

Cathcart's background gives the clue to his interest. He was a Scot, an Edinburgh man whose father was a close friend of Robert Louis Stevenson. After graduating in Edinburgh, young Cathcart decided to see a bit of the world and sailed to Australia and back in a sailing ship. But he suffered from a stammer in his speech and in order to try to cure it he took himself to Naples and became a pupil of Scafati, a teacher of the old *bel canto* method of singing. As a result of his studies with Scafati, Cathcart developed a passionate love of the human voice as a thing of beauty, quite apart from his professional knowledge of the mechanics of the throat from a medical point of view. And this care for the voice of the singer had a profound bearing on the start of the promenade concerts at Queen's Hall.

When in due course he met Newman and discussed the scheme, Cathcart agreed to put up some money – on two conditions. In order to avoid strain on singers' voices, the instruments of the orchestra must be tuned to the lower 'French' pitch instead of to the higher 'concert' pitch then customary here. And the conductor must be Henry J Wood, whose career Cathcart had been following since he heard him as a fourteen-year-old organist at a London exhibition.

Newman demurred on the question of making a change in the pitch of the orchestra. He saw no reason to change and, after all, there was the question of availability of the necessary wind instruments. As to

29

the choice of conductor, however, Newman does not seem to have required any persuasion. He, too, had been taking note of the progress of the young man who had once been his fellow student at the Royal Academy of Music, and he was wise enough to realise that here might well be just the man for the task that lay ahead.

Wood, on the other hand, agreed wholeheartedly with the suggestion that the lower pitch should be adopted; for even at that early age he had made himself an authority on the singing voice. Indeed, at the height of his fame years later he was to declare that he would just as gladly have spent his life as a teacher of singing as a conductor. That would have been a sad thing for the development of the appreciation of orchestral music in this country but, in fact, his knowledge of the art of singing had significant influence on one aspect of his talent as a conductor. He knew, for instance – and it is not by any means as platitudinous as it might seem – that a conductor must realise that a singer or a wind-player, in order to sing or play, must be permitted to carry out that basic process of breathing.

Eventually, agreement was reached on both points, but the immediate difficulty was, of course, that the wind instruments possessed by the players whom they would recruit for their orchestra would be tuned to the higher pitch. Dr Cathcart solved the problem by offering to buy instruments of the lower pitch out of his own pocket. These were in due course lent to the members of the orchestra, many of whom later bought them.

Dr George Cathcart certainly deserves his place in the story of the Proms, for he was an enthusiast who had faith. In the first season of the project, his faith cost him about £60 a night, something like £2,000 in all, but he never regretted it. One wonders, by the way, how many of the Prommers who gather round the fountain in the centre of the arena of the Royal Albert Hall know how and why it is there. It was Dr Cathcart's idea, just to freshen up the atmosphere of Queen's Hall, first with blocks of ice in the bowl and later with goldfish. Newman saw it as a way of breaking up the pressure of the crowd in the promenade, and, when the Proms moved in due course to the Albert Hall, the fountain was installed there too.

The fountain remains a typical part of the scene at the Proms, and, of course, Sir Thomas Beecham took the opportunity of making one of his little jokes about it. In a colourful description of the scene at the early Proms, he declared: 'Every three or four minutes some fascinating young female fell into the fountain and had to be rescued by a chivalrous swain. It must have happened thirty-five times every night. Foreigners came from all parts of Europe to see it'. That was a splendidly Beechamesque flourish, but in fact it was not until 1954 that Sir Thomas made his own personal début at the Proms. Dr Cathcart, at any rate, was able to say in his later years, 'You see, I was right in believing in the Proms – and my fountain is still there'. He was able to say that with genuine satisfaction, even though he found himself at the end of his life with hardly any money at all.

His practice in Upper Wimpole Street, where he had a fifteen-roomed house, was a lucrative one, and could have been much more so. But he did much of his highly skilled work for only nominal fees and, anyhow,

31

he saw no point in holding on to money for its own sake. He found it more rewarding to give it away. When, advanced in years, he *had* given it away and had sold the big house in Upper Wimpole Street, his fellow-specialists saw to it that he still had a room there and was well looked after. They gave him a dinner party to celebrate his ninetieth birthday not long before he died in 1951, almost fittingly, in a musicians' home.

For a personal impression of Dr Cathcart, I went to a former chorus girl named Marjorie Robertson.

'A wonderful man', she said. 'I was in the chorus of the Noël Coward revue, *This Year of Grace*, at the London Pavilion in 1928, when I suddenly developed a terribly sore throat. My doctor said that I must go and see Dr Cathcart, one of the leading specialists, in Upper Wimpole Street, but I pointed out that I couldn't afford to pay that kind of fee.

"Oh", said my doctor, "you don't have to worry about that. He loves the people in your profession and will do anything to help them. He will charge you only a nominal fee".

'I went to see Dr Cathcart and found him a short, spare man, then approaching seventy, in morning coat and wing collar. He took my tonsils out – and he charged me a fee that really *was* merely nominal.

'He was one of the leading men in his profession but he was immensely generous and gave most of his money away. He loved singers and was only too glad to use his skill and knowledge on their behalf.

'Not long before he died, I went to see him when he was living in a basement room in his old house in Upper Wimpole Street. He was surrounded by his books and his pictures and he looked *so* happy. I have never seen anyone who looked happier. He really was a dear old man.'

Such a man was Dr George Clark Cathcart, eminent physician, music-lover, and a pioneer influence in the founding of the Proms. And, by the way, the one-time chorus girl called Marjorie Robertson is rather better known today by another name – Anna Neagle!

4

YOUNG MISTER WOOD

THOUGH IT IS not recorded that the talented parents of Henry J Wood possessed the additional gift of being able to see what the future held in store, they might well have done so. Certainly they could hardly have chosen a more appropriate place for their only son's début on the world stage. He was born on 3rd March 1869, not far from the site of what was to be his main centre of activity, and the street, just off Oxford Street, was called, of all names, Newman Street. It was as though the Fates had decreed that his name and that of Newman were to be inseparably merged from the start of his life.

That particular significance could not have been foreseen by his parents, but clearly they did realise very soon the direction in which young Henry's future lay. Their own musical interests and talents provided fertile ground in which his own gifts might flourish; for his part Henry showed himself only too eager to derive full benefit from the encouragement they lavished upon him. Throughout his life he spoke of his parents with the deepest affection and with gratitude for all their efforts on his behalf.

Though neither of those parents was a professional musician, Henry must have had the sound of music ringing insistently in his ears from the time he first began to sit up and take notice. His Welsh-born mother had an attractive singing voice and a gift for teaching, and his father, who ran an optician's and model engineer's business, was a capable 'cellist, a pupil of John Hullah, and was for twenty-five years principal tenor at St Sepulchre's Church, Holborn Viaduct, the church at which there is held every year the service in celebration of the day of St Cecilia, the patron saint of music. Henry was taken to the church regularly and showed particular interest in the music of the organ, and today he is commemorated by a stained-glass window in the Musicians' Chapel there.

From his mother he 'learned his notes' and acquired the interest in singing that was to be a major influence in his life. From the age of six he could play the piano part in works by Bach and Haydn with his father and friends, and a little later he was also playing the violin and viola. Even as a youngster he was as much a glutton for work and a striver after knowledge and perfection as he was to be in the strenuous years that lay ahead.

He made rapid progress at the piano and organ and by the time he was ten he was sometimes acting as deputy organist at St Mary Aldermanbury. Four years later, by then a boy with piercing blue eyes and a mop of jet black hair and so small in stature that his feet barely reached the pedals, 'Master Henry J Wood' was giving recitals at the Fisheries Exhibition – where Dr Cathcart first heard him – and a couple of years later at the Inventions Exhibition. His experience as a performer began very early indeed, and he always said that he never suffered from nerves when appearing before the public, undoubtedly because he was so meticulous in preparing his work. Throughout his career he left nothing to chance or to some hoped-for 'inspiration' of the moment. All was carefully planned in advance down to the last detail.

Two years were spent at the Royal Academy of Music – with which he was to maintain a close association throughout his life – and, apart from his own studies, which earned him four Gold Medals, he was kept very busy and acquired valuable experience as accompanist to the singing and operatic classes conducted by a number of distinguished professors. At about this time, in addition, he was appointed organist and choirmaster at St John's Church, Fulham.

All the time he was busily acquiring new organ music and orchestral scores. He burnt much midnight oil as he pored over them, studying and annotating, and laying the foundation for the exhaustive private music library which he was to build up through the years and which is now housed in the Royal Academy of Music. He was also seizing every opportunity of studying eminent conductors at work, and, whenever possible, his father arranged for him to go over to the Continent to widen his experience of their different method. Not surprisingly, he could discourse at length on their contrasting stick-techniques.

As at any time in Henry Wood's life, there might well have been a touch of sarcasm in the tone of voice of anyone asking him: 'And what do you do in your spare time?' In fact, his 'spare' time was mostly spent in painting – he studied at St John's Wood School of Art and later at the Slade – and such was his talent in that direction that, if music had not dominated his life, he might have established an independent reputation as a painter. Some fine oils of his are now in the Henry Wood Memorial Room at the Royal Academy of Music. When his spare time was not occupied in painting, he was likely to be busy at carpentry or going off on long rides on his bicycle.

From an early age he was determined to make himself master of the technique of the singing voice, not because he saw for himself a career as a singer, but in order that he might be fully equipped as a teacher and accompanist. He worked with seventeen different teachers of singing, though he once said that only two of them, Duvivier and Manuel Garcia, were much good. Indeed, it was the famed Garcia who said to him: 'Henry, don't you ever dare to sing in public. You haven't an operatic voice. You have a conductor's voice – the kind that would go through a brick wall'.

Be that as it may, backed by detailed expert knowledge, Wood had a remarkable talent for teaching others just how they could make the most effective use of such vocal equipment as they possessed. Here the practical side of his nature made him an admirable teacher; for, though he was an artist of the utmost sensitivity, his feet were firmly planted on the ground. It was sound practical sense that he talked to his pupils, with constant stress on the importance of hard work, self-discipline, and physical well-being. His special knowledge of the technique of singing – he wrote an exhaustive four-volume treatise on *The Gentle Art of Singing*[1] – enabled him to be an unusually fine accompanist. As a young man he did a great deal of work of this sort and, even in later life when he was otherwise too heavily engaged to undertake such

[1] *The Gentle Art of Singing*, Henry Wood, Oxford UP.

activities, he was often offered high fees by leading artists who wished him to join them.

A typical instance of his down-to-earth and practical way of giving advice is provided by his words to a big choir which he was training for a festival occasion: 'Arrange your mouths before you put on your voices. Regulate your breathing and don't blow. I loathe people who take breath like a vacuum cleaner. The greatest singers in the world don't open their mouths wide but, by Jove! they open their throats. Take my tip and don't go too often to the aquarium'.

Talking of singers reminds us of one of the many stories that Henry Wood enjoyed telling. It concerned an inexpert compère (as we would call him today) who forgot to make an announcement before one of the singers began, but hastened to do so immediately after the song.

'Ladies and gentlemen', he said, 'Mr Blank asked me to apologise for his voice before he sang. I omitted to do this and so I - er - apologise now'.

At nineteen, Wood applied himself intensively to gaining experience as a conductor and it was in opera, in a tour with the Arthur Rouseby Opera Company, that he plunged in, so to speak, at the deep end. Experience of the tough sort it certainly was, for in the provinces he often had to do the best he could with scratch orchestras, many of whose players were totally unfamiliar with the music they were called upon to tackle. It was uphill work, full of frustrations, but he was learning all the time.

When the company visited one Lancashire town, the flute player had fallen ill and the manager of the theatre volunteered to get a local substitute. But, to the conductor's horror, the man missed cues all over the place and, as though to compensate for his lapses, threw in showers of wrong notes. At the first interval Wood went up to the fellow and burst out: 'I thought you could play the flute!'

'So did I', was the reply. 'It's been a bit of a suck-in for both of us, owd laad!'

After conducting the Carl Rosa Opera Company in a farewell tour by the French soprano Marie Roze, whom he greatly admired (she had been the first to sing Manon in London and was also a notable Carmen and Marguerite), Wood assisted Sullivan and D'Oyly Carte in rehearsals of *The Yeoman of the Guard* at the Savoy Theatre, and also superintended the rehearsals of Sullivan's serious opera, *Ivanhoe*, at the Royal English Opera House, which D'Oyly Carte had just built in Cambridge Circus. It is now the Palace Theatre.

Of even greater significance, however, was his appointment by Signor Lago to conduct an opera season at the Olympic Theatre, off the Strand – significant because he was concerned there with the first production in this country of Tchaikovsky's opera, *Eugene Onegin*, which stimulated his interest in this composer and in Russian music generally. The results of this were to be found in Prom programmes in which he introduced to this country many Russian works now firmly established in the orchestral repertoire. During a visit to Bayreuth he struck up a valuable acquaintance with the eminent conductor Felix Mottl, who had worked with Wagner; and, by way of variety, he conducted a musical comedy called *The Lady Slavey* in London's West End.

When Robert Newman made the fateful choice of Henry Wood as the central figure in the Proms enterprise at Queen's Hall, he picked a man with precisely the qualities he was looking for. Wood was young and bubbling with enthusiasm and vitality; he possessed a positive and engaging personality; he was not yet very well-known to the general public and thus, assuming that the scheme were successful, his steadily growing reputation would be linked with that of the Proms and would imbue that 'personal' character to the proceedings; his technical knowledge was remarkable; and, for his age, he had already acquired impressively wide experience. He had, for instance, conducted some fifty different operas and, though opera was not to be the main feature of the Proms, that experience alone was enormously valuable in his task of handling orchestra and soloists.

Not by any means of least importance in an enterprise which involved the planning and carrying through of continuous series of concerts were his abounding energy and his orderly and methodical way of going about things. It is true that Wood suffered from what was at that time a serious disadvantage. He had been so misguided as to be born and trained in England. In the then musical climate in this country foreign names were the fashion. It was hardly believable that a young Englishman could actually be the equal of someone with a resounding foreign name, and as for an Englishman conducting Wagner, well, well! This idea was to persist to some extent for very many years – Wood had his own little joke about it in the 'Klenovsky' episode some time later – but, as things turned out, he was to prove to be the very man to win such esteem and

41

acclaim as to break down many of the barriers of prejudice. He was the forerunner of a distinguished line of native conductors, many of whom were themselves to be associated with the Queen's Hall Orchestra and with the Proms during their careers. Basil Cameron, Sir John Barbirolli, and the late Sir Eugene Goossens, to mention only three, were all at some time members of the orchestra under Henry Wood.

The first task for the creators of the Proms was to bring together a full-scale symphony orchestra of high quality, not by any means an easy task in those days when orchestral playing was a somewhat casual occupation. At that time there were only two other permanent orchestras in the country – the Crystal Palace Orchestra, which had been giving concerts for forty years under August Manns, and the Hallé Orchestra, established in Manchester in 1857. There was no permanent symphony orchestra in central London, in contrast to the present day when, in London alone, there are five symphony orchestras of first-class quality – the BBC, the London Philharmonic, the London Symphony, the New Philharmonia, and the Royal Philharmonic – and several other important ensembles, as well as fine orchestras in other centres.

With their customary thoroughness, Wood and Newman set about assembling their forces. Through the artists' entrance to Queen's Hall there passed a steady stream of applicants – many of them foreigners – carrying every kind of orchestral instrument and eager for the chance of a job with a permanent orchestra. Not long after the Proms had started, Wood typically established a regular procedure whereby he set aside one day a month for the testing of instrumentalists who wished to join his orchestra. In one year he listened to nearly nine hundred different players.

Sir Eugene Goossens gave a lively account in *Overture and Beginners*[1] of his own experience in auditioning for the Queen's Hall Orchestra in 1912, when he was nineteen:

> Wood was a bit ruffled when at the start of the audition the D string on my violin snapped with a resounding bang, completely unnerving me for some time. 'Dear, dear; a fine time to break a string', he said. 'And I've *so* much to do. Brown, send in Mr X, please.'
>
> I left to get a new string, and returned just in time to hear through the door the horrible sounds Mr X was making in his attempts to read at sight *The Ride of the Valkyries*. He soon emerged, pale and visibly shaken, and I took his place.
>
> First I played part of a concerto, then 'Read that' in a tone of voice from Henry J that boded ill for me if I failed. 'That' proved to be something from *Parsifal* – hideously slow, so that my bow shook. This was followed by a *scherzando* movement with rapidly alternating changes of time, all to be played *spiccato*, by some composer I can't think of. Then a manuscript piece which I flunked, causing Wood to murmur, 'Dear, dear, dear!' And so on and so forth, until with the perspiration pouring down and my knees shaking, and feeling like a victim stretched on the rack, I heard:
>
> 'Are there any more outside, Brown?' 'No, Mr Wood, them's all', and H J saying to me then: 'Go and tell Mr Newman you're engaged. First violin. Very good indeed. But watch those MS sheets. Dear, dear, dear: we constantly play new works. All from MS parts. Practise reading manuscript all the time. Dear me, watch those MSS!'

[1] *Overture and Beginners*, Eugene Goossens, Methuen & Co.

Thus began a four-year association with a fine conductor and an outstanding orchestra. In the service of both I spent invaluable years of apprenticeship, and got a first-hand knowledge of practically the entire symphonic repertory. Under no other conductor could a more thorough and authentic grounding in the orchestral repertory have been obtained, and certainly no conductor of that day combined better musicianship with a finer stick-technique than did Wood.

Even though I played under other men with greater 'box office' names than H J W (Nikisch, Mengelberg, Steinberg, Safonoff), I never encountered a sincerer artist or a more resourceful, experienced and versatile conductor than the beloved head of the Queen's Hall Orchestra. The debt owed him by the last two generations of English composers alone is a fantastic one, and that of the British public to him is incalculable. It is largely due to his efforts that appreciation and understanding – such as it is – of that public for the meatier things in the contemporary symphonic repertory exist at all.

It is indicative of the state of music in London in 1895 that, in the first orchestra to play at the Proms, many of the principal players were foreigners – the first flute, Dutch; first oboe, French; first clarinet, Spanish; and first horn, German.

Little could the eighty members of that orchestra – soon to be increased to a hundred – have realised what a shock they were in for. They were to find themselves under the rigid discipline of a man who was a model of self-discipline. They were to say goodbye to the casual days when it was the recognised thing for orchestral players to stroll in ten minutes or so after a rehearsal was due to begin. No longer was it to be possible to slip out for a couple of quick half-pints at their

44

favourite caravanserai, *The George*, which they were to learn to call 'The Gluepot'.

They could not, of course, know that in fifty years' time Ralph Vaughan Williams would be saying: 'Any good orchestral playing in England now is due to the early work of Henry Wood'. And they would find it hard to realise that, before very long, they would be returning the very genuine affection that this 'tyrant', Henry J Wood, felt for them.

While recruiting their orchestra, Wood and Newman had to apply themselves to planning the programmes for their first season. It was not the elaborate jigsaw affair it is today; for, whereas a great number of solo singers and instrumentalists appear in the course of a present-day season, the early policy was to use a small group of soloists, some of whom appeared in several different concerts. But there were the particular problems of the time, one of them being that the major burden of the season would have to be carried by one man and one orchestra.

Undoubtedly, Wood would have been happier to make the programme content more substantial right from the start, but he admired and trusted Newman's lively business sense and he deferred, perhaps reluctantly, to a scheme whereby the first programmes would contain many items of the lightest sort, similar to those of the promenade concerts to which the London public had become accustomed. But these were the sprats with which they hoped to catch the mackerel.

In a very short time, Prommers who had come to hear the usual light offerings would be finding that they were getting symphonies and substantial operatic

45

excerpts. They would be discussing the merits of Tchaikovsky, or becoming familiar with long passages by Wagner ('bleeding chunks of Wagner' they would be called by adverse critics), or encountering Debussy and a hitherto unknown fellow called Mahler and such bewildering composers as Schoenberg and Bartók.

What is more, they would find themselves liking them. Well, perhaps not always, at first. There was to be the gentleman who, on first experiencing an excerpt from Wagner's *Tristan and Isolde* at a Prom, would call out, disgustedly, 'Rot!' and bustle out of Queen's Hall, followed by the withering eye of Henry Wood. And there was to be the famed hissing of Schoenberg's *Five Orchestral Pieces*.

But it was in fact the calculated build-up of a loyal audience for music of the better and at the time often unfamiliar sort that differentiated the Proms from most of the similar ventures that had gone before. It was a matter of giving audiences what they wanted, while at the same time placing before them much that they would find themselves wanting in the years to come. There was no accident about it. Through the years, the Proms have always been planned. The plan has changed with the times, but a plan there has always been. And so, while other enterprises faded out, the Proms have gone on.

5

MUSIC — AND THE MOVIES

THE POTTED PALMS were in place and the flowers, always to be a pleasant feature of the Proms, gave a festive air to the occasion. In the promenade were the stalls where you could buy for yourself a cigar, for your lady a flower, or for both of you an ice-cream at the 'Horton Ice Stall'. But if you were in the mood for a drink, you must wait until the interval, or at least until the end of one of the items, before you could repair to one of the bars in Queen's Hall. Cigars, flowers and ice-cream were all very well, for they could be enjoyed without causing noisy interruption, but the sound of popping champagne corks, which had become too much of a good thing at some other promenade concerts, must be confined to its proper place.

Prices of admission were deliberately kept at a modest level, for it was important to attract a wide and varied public. The object of developing the musical taste of the audience could be achieved only if the audience could be induced to attend. It cost one shilling for admission to the promenade or balcony, and half-a-crown for a Grand Circle seat, numbered and reserved. Season tickets were one guinea for the promenade, two guineas for the balcony, and three and five guineas for the Grand Circle.

The twopenny programme, a large singly-folded

47

sheet, contained much miscellaneous information, apart from the actual musical items. Two firms of tailors were eager to sell you 'Evening Dress (lined through-out silk)' from £5, and Pagani's Restaurant in Great Portland Street, which was to be closely linked with the Proms until Hitler's bombers decided otherwise, was ready to welcome you after the concert.

In bold type in the programme was this announce-ment: 'At these concerts the French Pitch (Diapason Normal) will exclusively be used. Mr Newman is glad to say that it will also be adopted in future by the Philharmonic Society, The Bach Choir, The London Symphony, Mottl and Nikisch Concerts, and also the concerts under his direction, i e The Queen's Hall Choir, and the Sunday Afternoon Orchestral Concerts.' Dr Cathcart's influence had made itself felt.

The orchestra did not yet boast a name of its own. It was simply 'Full Orchestra', led by W Frye Parker. H Lane Wilson, whose name many people will remember as a writer of ballads, was the piano accompanist. Programme notes were by Edgar F Jacques.

The house was crowded, many of those present probably having looked in out of curiosity to see what was going on. And on the dot of eight o'clock on this evening of 10th August 1895, young Mr Henry J Wood, his full black beard suggesting more than his twenty-six years, made his way on to the platform, looked down for the first time at the upturned faces of the Prommers, raised his long baton, and launched his first season of Promenade Concerts. It was signifi-cant that the very first item should be by Wagner — the *Rienzi* overture.

48

The two men who inspired the Promenade Concerts: Robert Newman (*Left*) who inaugurated the concerts at Queen's Hall, London, in 1895, and Sir Henry Wood (*Below*) after whom the concerts are named.

Before Robert Newman
established the Proms,
concerts were known as
Promenades and had
been staged for some
years under that name in
London's Vauxhall
Gardens (*Above*).   The
idea of appointing one
conductor for a series of
concerts was also not
new.   The flamboyant
Louis Jullien (*Right*) was
the sole conductor at the
English Opera House in
Drury Lane.

The programme, a decidedly mixed bag, would raise an indulgent smile from the much more sophisticated Prommers of today but it was deliberately so, designed to draw in and hold an audience and to lay the modest foundation for the great things that were to come.

After the overture, Mr Ffrangcon-Davies sang the *Pagliacci* Prologue, followed by two orchestral items, Chabrier's *Habañera* and Chopin's *Polonaise in A*, orchestrated by Glazounov. Madame Marie Duma then obliged with 'Swiss Song' by Eckert. There were flute solos by Mr A Fransella – Benjamin Godard's *Idylle* and *Valse* – and Mr Ivor McKay sang 'Since thou hast come' by Kenningham.

Chromatic Concert Valses from the opera *Eulenspiegel* by Cyrill Kistler (described in the programme as 'one of the most promising of living German composers') may not give the present-day concert-goer much of a thrill but it was a 'First London performance', the first of the 'novelties' which have been an important feature of the Proms from the earliest days.

Mrs Van Der Veer-Green sang Saint-Saëns' 'My heart at thy sweet voice', the orchestra played Ambroise Thomas's *Mignon Gavotte*, Mr W A Peterkin contributed 'Vulcan's Song' from Gounod's *Philémon et Baucis*, and the orchestra brought the first half to a close with a flourish in Liszt's *Hungarian Rhapsody in D Minor and G Minor* (*No.* 2).

After an interval of fifteen minutes, the second half went like this:

| Grand Selection | *Carmen* | Bizet (Arranged by Cellier) |

Song	'Largo al factotum' (*Il Barbiere*) Mr Ffrancon-Davies	Rossini
Overture	*Mignon*	Ambroise Thomas
Solo cornet	*Serenade* Mr Howard Reynolds	Schubert
Song	'My mother bids me bind my hair' Madame Marie Duma	Haydn
Solo Bassoon	'Lucy Long' Mr E F James	
Song	'Dear Heart' Mr Ivor McKay	Tito Mattei
	'The Uhlan's Call'	Eilenberg
Song	'Loch Lomond' Mrs Van Der Veer-Green	Old Scottish
Song	'A Soldier's Song' Mr W A Peterkin	Mascheroni
Valse	*Amoretten Tanze*	Gungl
Grand March	*Les Enfants de la Garde* (First performance)	Schloesser (Orch Harold Vickars)

Even though that first programme seems, to our eyes, to be a strange collection of bits and pieces, it is worth examination. Though it would hardly have the crowds clamouring at the box-office nowadays, it was designed for its time and with shrewd purpose behind it. The items were easy on the ear – nothing to frighten anybody away. There were two 'novelties' – a première of the arrangement of Schloesser's Grand March and a first London performance of Kistler's Valses. The

Rienzi overture provided a hint of Henry Wood's determination to familiarise his Prom audiences with the sound of Wagner. And the ballads were in keeping with the time when, in the days before radio and television, people were accustomed to enjoying 'musical evenings' at home.

The programme, not all that unlike those of the promenade concerts that had been presented in other places, was, so to speak, a 'trailer' to what was to come. Both Wood and Newman were much too wise to tell their popular public that they were embarking on a series of 'educational' concerts. The term might well have sounded forbidding. But that is precisely what they were doing.

The modern concert-goer might think that he could get along nicely without Mr Howard Reynolds and his solo cornet but in fact that item was one of the most popular in the early Proms. Mr Reynolds was there throughout the first season, and for some time later, with such offerings as 'Love's Old Sweet Song', 'For all eternity', 'Killarney', and 'The Lost Chord'. Indeed, on the Last Night of that opening season, he not only rendered 'For all eternity' but, laying aside his cornet, blew a rollicking 'Post Horn Galop' to top things off. And he was given prominent billing for the fact that he would be taking part in the Sunday afternoon Grand Orchestral Concerts starting on the following day.

It all sounds rather naïve today, but one cannot help having a soft spot for Mr Reynolds – by all accounts a fine player – as one thinks of him giving his cornet a final, loving polish before setting out, night after night, from his home in Richmond. For he was one of the first stars of the Proms. Mr A Fransella, principal flute in the orchestra and a frequent soloist, was another.

The attraction of the cornet was not, by the way, confined to the solo performances of Mr Reynolds. In one early season the Park Sisters appeared regularly – and they were a cornet quartet!

Even in that first season of the Proms a sort of pattern began to emerge. On the fourth night the term 'Classical Night' was first used in the billing of a programme which included Beethoven's *King Stephen* overture and Schubert's *Unfinished* Symphony. Wagner already began to loom large on the Prom scene, an early concert being mainly devoted to his music, including a substantial excerpt from *Die Meistersinger*. Monday was becoming his night, just as Friday was later to become Beethoven's. Complete first halves of programmes were devoted to Mendelssohn (including his *Italian* Symphony), Gounod, Schubert, and the Strauss family. And Mr Wood certainly went to town with one 'Novelty Night', the programme including six English premières (among them Richard Strauss's Prelude to Act 1 of *Guntram*, Svendsen's *Andante Funèbre*, and Tchaikovsky's *Marche Solenelle*); two London premières (including Massenet's *Phèdre* Overture); and two world premières.

In studying those early programmes, all of them in bound volumes in the BBC's Music Library, one gets a sense of sharing in the thoughts of Wood and Newman as they worked out their plans for the betterment of music in London.

The first season created a favourable impression and at the end of it *The Musical Times* had this to say of the young conductor: 'In Mr Henry J Wood a highly intelligent and experienced conductor has been secured and he now has his forces well under control. Although conductors are said to be born, not made, occasion is an important factor in their development. These concerts have proved to be Mr Wood's opportunity and have served to show that he possesses exceptional ability.'

Always on the look-out for extra attractions for his audiences, Robert Newman introduced a new idea – a 'gimmick', if you like – into his second season of Proms. During the interval and again at the end of the concert, were to be seen 'Animated Photographs' in Queen's Hall's small hall, which held five hundred people. Perhaps puffing a 'Flor di Dindigul', bought at the Cigar Stall for threepence, the concert-goer would pay an extra sixpence to see the pictures, 'reproduced with all the actual movements of real life', presented by David Devant, whom many people will still remember as the famous conjurer of the Maskelyne and Devant partnership.

There would seem to be a certain tameness in such subjects as 'Up the River', 'Margate Sands', 'Cycling in the Park', and 'Arrival of a Railway Train', though an element of sex broke in with 'Ladies Drilling'. These picture-shows continued for several seasons and the material became rather more exciting; for instance, 'Scenes at a Spanish Bullfight – Arrival of Toreadors – In the Arena – Bull Goring the Horses' ('The above are retained owing to their immense popularity').

It is difficult to guess at what might have been contained in such an episode as 'Spanish method of raising War Funds', but 'A Phantom Ride on the

South-Eastern through Kent' might strike a topical note for commuters of today. The South African War brought such excerpts as 'A war balloon and train crossing the Vaal River' and 'A skirmish with the Boers near Kimberley by a party of General French's cavalry scouts'. These were shown in the same programme with 'The Yellow Peril', though the nerves of patrons were later steadied by 'Macaroni-eating competition', 'Polytechnic Harriers' Paper Chase', and 'Incoming Tide at Worthing'.

Smoking has been allowed at the Proms from earliest days but, after a few seasons, Mr Newman was impelled to make this announcement: 'Smoking is permitted at these Concerts, excepting in the seats between doors E and F in the Grand Circle, which are reserved for non-smokers. Gentlemen are politely requested to refrain from striking matches during the performance of the various items'.

As part of the old tradition, smoking is still permitted in the Proms of today, but few people take advantage of the fact – either because they do not know that smoking *is* permitted or, more likely, because they have got round to the idea that smoking in a hall in which artists are performing is not a good thing. Anyone who has attended a boxing-match in the Royal Albert Hall and has observed the proceedings through a heavy pall of smoke will have realised that, if Prom audiences really applied themselves to the weed, that old easy-going custom would have to be changed.

After the interval, I have seen young fellows finishing off a cigarette and being told by a helpful steward, 'It's all right, sir, you can smoke inside', but choosing to have the last few puffs before going to their seats. It's better that way.

In studying the early programmes, one gets a sense of the changing times in which the concerts were presented. In a programme of 1896, for instance, Queen Victoria is described as 'the friend of Mendelssohn and the first Englishwoman to recognise the genius of Wagner', and there is this addition, 'When Queen Victoria ascended the throne, Exeter Hall was the only building available for concerts on a large scale. Things musical have changed since then, and it is particularly appropriate that the longest reign in British history should be celebrated in a Hall named after Her Majesty, and itself one of the latest and most conspicuous signs of that change'.

Mr Newman never missed a chance for a celebration. An instance of his adroitness in seizing upon a topical event in order to attract patrons to his promenade concerts is provided by the *America's* Cup yacht race of 1899, when Sir Thomas Lipton's *Shamrock* challenged the American yacht *Columbia*.

The Prom audience was given this information:

'The issue is expected to be known in London in the course of this evening's programme. Mr Robert Newman has made special arrangements for the result to be at once communicated to Queen's Hall. The name of the winning yacht will be announced from the platform at the earliest possible moment, and the orchestra will play a few bars of "Rule Britannia" or "Hail Columbia" according to the event. If the *Shamrock* should, as he hopes, prove successful, Mr Newman begs the audience, as a favour, to allow the programme to be at once proceeded with after the

55

bars of ''Rule Britannia'' have been played, as there will be another opportunity for the display of national enthusiasm in Part II, at the end of the Fantasia, *Reminiscences of England*.'

Sadly, Mr Newman's fears of a prolonged display of national enthusiasm were unfounded. He had to settle for a few bars of 'Hail Columbia.'

Those were the trimmings and side-issues that helped to draw attention to the Proms in the early days, but the really important thing was that Henry Wood and Robert Newman were busy all the time on their work of making their programmes more fully representative of the available repertoire. They were introducing new artists, many of them just starting their careers, providing a platform for new works by British and foreign composers, giving more substantial scenes from, in particular, the operas of Wagner, performing a widening range of the standard classics, and presenting many works which today come into the 'standard' category but which were then unknown to London audiences. One gathers that one matter on which Wood and Newman did not see eye to eye in the early days was the inclusion of the music of Bach. Wood wished to give a fuller representation of it, but Newman suspected it might at that stage be box-office 'poison'. In due course, however, Bach was more substantially represented and an enthusiastic following built up.

Wood was always sharply aware of trends in contemporary music and it is worth remembering that many composers who are 'classics' to present-day audiences were contemporaries or near contemporaries when he was performing their works in the early years of the Proms. For instance, when the Proms started in

1895, Verdi was 82, Brahms 62, Saint-Saëns 60, Balakirev 58, Dvorak 54, Massenet 53, Grieg 52, Rimsky-Korsakov and Sarasate 51, Fauré 50, Liadov 40, Elgar 38, Mahler 35, Debussy 33, Richard Strauss 31, Sibelius and Glazounov 30, Vaughan Williams 23, and Rachmaninov only 22. Chabrier and Anton Rubinstein had been dead only one year, Tchaikovsky two years, César Franck five years, Liszt nine years, and Wagner twelve years.

6

'TIMBER'

I T WOULD NOT be true to say that Henry Wood –
Sir Henry, as he became in 1911 – ever really walked
on to a concert platform. His progress was more in the
nature of an eager little trot, rather as though he were
anxious that his reputation for punctuality should not
be marred and that he and his friends in the audience
should proceed to have a jolly good time together as
soon as possible.

White carnation in his lapel – his was the *first* white
carnation at the Proms – he would acknowledge the
welcoming applause with a quick sweep of the arm,
which would embrace the orchestra as well as the
audience, and then, without further fuss, he would
raise his baton.

On the advice of Richter, one of the conductors whom
he admired, he always used a long baton, made to his
own design and carefully balanced, with a substantial
cork handle, and painted white so as to show up
clearly against his black coat. And, as that baton made
its first move downwards, the clocks in the world
outside Queen's Hall would be striking eight.

It was not long before he acquired an affectionate
nickname, first among members of the orchestra and
later among the audience; and the chosen nickname,
'Timber', could hardly have been more appropriate,

not only for its play on his own name but also for its suggestion of staunchness and reliability.

It used to be said that nothing but an earthquake would make 'Timber' late for a rehearsal or a concert, and it did in fact take a taxi-cab crash to make him late on the only recorded occasion at a Prom. But he got there, bandaged and twenty minutes after time – and no doubt furious. There was the other occasion when he was *thought* to be late. It was actually two minutes after eight o'clock when he raised his baton and many in the audience began to wonder, in a state of consternation, whether 'Old Timber' was perhaps getting slack – until it was realised that the BBC had then begun to broadcast the concerts and had specifically asked Sir Henry to start at two minutes past eight so that they might make their opening announcement on the air at eight o'clock. His cherished reputation was saved.

Wood began his conductorship of the Proms exactly as he intended to go on, planning all his work like an elaborate military operation down to the last detail of preliminary preparation, rehearsal, and performance. He not only worked through his own score bar by bar, marking various points in his famous blue pencil, but he also insisted upon going through each band part separately. All this involved enormous labour and concentration but he never forgot that, as a very young man, he once discovered at eleven o'clock at night that there was a whole bar wrong in his copies of Beethoven's *Pastoral Symphony*.

With the knowledge of breathing he had acquired in his studies of singing, he marked in his score the points at which the singer or instrumentalist should take breath and, as a result of this care and thought for the performer, he was as fine an accompanist when holding the baton as he was when seated at the piano. During the performance of a vocal work or of a concerto, he would always have a watchful eye on the mouth of the singer, the hands of the pianist, or the fingers of the violinist. Indications of phrasing and bowing were all marked in his score and he would also write out amazingly detailed instructions about method of performance. For instance, in a score of Bach's *B Minor Mass* for performance in Sheffield as far back as 1911, he gave guidance of this sort:

'Second soprano. "Gloria". Sing most of this number with a smiling position of the lips and mouth, as, by this means, forwardness, brightness of tone, and ring can be obtained and maintained. Never let the first syllable in the word "Gloria" approach "Gloo", and always pronounce the second syllable of the word "ex-cel-sis" with great forced accent, and be quite sure that it tells to the public as "chael" and not "sell".'

Or this: 'Bass. "Et Resurrexit". Get the tone very bright and metallic; do not contract the eyebrows or even look fierce, but sing with real exultation, with the greatest vitality and brilliancy, getting the words in the teeth, the tone to be open, never dull, confidential or covered; and, most of all, sing it from memory and look the audience straight in the face'.

That was the sheer practical way in which he approached everything he did. In his library at the Royal Academy of Music is his own edition of *Messiah*, a monster score showing on each page Handel's music arranged for small orchestra and choir, then for larger

61

forces, and finally for a gargantuan ensemble. One would imagine that the last of these versions was most after his own heart for, in a work of this nature, he loved a big and generous sound.

As far back as 1902, Henry Wood was addressing choristers in these terms:

'Words – words are our masters. When you go to hear a bad opera at the theatre and listen with rapt attention to the principal comedian, what attracts you? You are able without effort to hear every word he sings – herein lies the pleasure. You forget that he has no voice.

'Now think, when you are singing choruses, what a delight to the public it will be if they can hear every word. Also, I want your faces to portray the whole range of emotion contained in the words you are singing. I must impress upon you that, unless the nerve current sent from the brain to express feeling or emotion is shown upon the countenance, the vocal mechanism will be unable adequately to give effect to the expression intended by the words.

'All sincere emotion is expressed in facial nerve thrills. The meaning of uttered words should be written on every face, for, unless you can express feeling and emotion in your face, you cannot express feeling and emotion in the tones of your voice. Your attention and anxiety must not be centred on mere notes. Try to sing words of scorn with an absolutely impassive face! You cannot do it – your voice will belie your words. See to it that you are living and that you have human pulses beating'.

Right up to the time when, in 1927, the BBC took over the Proms, Wood had only three three-hour rehearsals for the six concerts of each week, starting precisely at ten o'clock and finishing on the dot of one o'clock – and what severely shook the orchestral players in the early days was the fact that a rehearsal timed for ten o'clock should actually *start* at that time. This was something which, from all their experience up to date, they had not bargained for. What was more, even before the start of the rehearsal, they had to take part in a solemn routine which became known as Wood's 'tuning parade'.

Wood was a great one for precise pitch and every player had to file past him and satisfy him that his instrument was in tune. For this purpose he first used an electric tuning-fork but, finding that it did not go on sounding long enough for his purpose, he devised another piece of apparatus, worked by a handle, on the principle of an organ-pipe. It had a small wind-chest containing three little sets of bellows, each of which relieved the next as they successively ran out of breath. It remained absolutely in tune for years.

The players hated it, but Dame Ethel Smyth, the composer, was immensely impressed and waxed quite lyrical about it: 'The twenty minutes' procession before that box, man after man, dominated by its soft, insistent voice, is to my mind a strangely impressive sight – ritualistic, almost sacrificial, and reminiscent somehow of the Elgin Marbles frieze. But the system finds no imitators, for, if it is not to be a farce, the conductor must be on the spot, like a general at a review, half an hour before the battle begins.'

The players who took part in the procession tended to describe it in more down-to-earth and decidedly

63

less poetic terms and without any allusion to the Elgin Marbles!

It is said, by the way, that one day a group of 'cellists played a little joke that Henry Wood never spotted. They duly filed past to have their 'A' checked and were told either 'a little up' or 'a little down'; but what they did not reveal was that they were passing the same cello from one to another!

If the players were not long in finding the apt name of 'Timber' for their conductor, he on his part very soon discovered the presence of the tavern called The George, just round the corner at the junction of Mortimer Street and Great Portland Street—not because he frequented it but because it was a favourite haunt of his players. He proceeded to give it a new name. Noting that some of the orchestra were missing from the ranks one day, he muttered, 'I expect they're stuck in that Gluepot round the corner'. And 'The Gluepot' it has been to musicians ever since.

Rehearsals were hard work all the time, without the waste of a minute – they had to be if he was to get through the task before him – but Wood never kept the orchestra after one o'clock unless some really urgent problem had arisen. Then he would say: 'Gentlemen, do you think you could spare me another half-hour?' The amount of time to be devoted to rehearsing each work was precisely marked in his schedule, and on his desk, or sometimes on the floor at his feet, would be placed his famous 'turnip' watch, whereby he could check exactly how things were going.

This strict time-keeping was a boon to the many composers whose works were given first performances at the Proms, for they knew in advance exactly when

Three leading personalities in the life of the Promenade Concerts: (*Right*) Basil Cameron, the first associate conductor, who was awarded the OBE in 1957, (*Below Left*) the British composer and conductor, Constant Lambert and (*Below Right*) William Glock, who was appointed BBC Controller of Music in 1959 and whose duties include the planning and preparation of each Promenade Concert Season.

Men of the baton at the Proms: Sir Henry Wood, Sir John Barbirolli, Sir Malcolm Sargent and Colin Davis.

their piece was going to be rehearsed. If they wished, Wood always encouraged them to conduct their own works but, as composers are not by any means always the best conductors even of their own pieces, he was always there to give generous advice on how the composer-conductor could best obtain the result he desired.

There was also Henry Wood's little hand-bell. Sometimes he would leave the leader of the orchestra to carry on with the rehearsal while he disappeared into the open spaces of the house to satisfy himself on matters of acoustics and balance. A tinkle of the bell would check the proceedings and the voice from 'outer space'—maybe some recess of the balcony—would point out in its Cockney-type accent just how the fault should be corrected.

Despite the intensity of these rehearsals, there were, of course, occasions when 'cheerfulness would keep breaking in'. If things were not going quite as they should, Wood had a way of saying, querulously, 'What are you a-doin' of?' But there came the time when he simply asked, 'What are you a-doin'?' – and with one voice the orchestra sang out the single word, 'OF!'

On another occasion, some of the players who were for the moment unoccupied were having a few furtive puffs at cigarettes. Without looking up from his score, Wood chided them: 'I can see smoke emerging from behind your music-stands. I thought the only people who smoked on the job were taxi-drivers'. It happened that the soloist of the day was Benno Moiseiwitsch who, as was his regular procedure at rehearsal, took off his jacket, fitted a cigarette into his long holder, lit up, and took his seat at the piano. Immediately there was a hearty yell from the orchestra: 'Taxi!' It was not until after the rehearsal that they were able to explain to the bewildered Moiseiwitsch what all the excitement was about.

Wood never conducted without a score – understandably, when one considers the huge variety of music he performed night after night during a Proms season and in view of his insistence on leaving nothing to chance. But, if he had been asked, he might well have given the retort of the German conductor, Hans Knappertsbusch, when he was asked why he never conducted from memory, as did so many other conductors. 'Why should I?' demanded Knappertsbusch. 'I can read a score.'

There seems to be no doubt that Henry Wood actually enjoyed rehearsing. As he once said: 'The pleasure of conducting does not lie in the actual performance but in the preparation of the performance – the pulling together of the whole thing. This is the conductor's view of the situation: the players' opinion is the opposite. It is a peculiarity of choruses and instrumentalists that they don't like rehearsals. They love best the conductor who gives them the least work'. Yet no conductor has been more sincerely loved by the people who worked with him than was Henry Wood.

He could not stand choristers whose looks wandered round the hall or who buried their noses in their books. 'Every eye on the conductor', he would command. 'I don't want to see anybody fidgeting or talking or waving to friends. If I do, I shall take a cab and go home'. And he would proceed to teach them to sing far better than they ever thought they could.

During an orchestral rehearsal, Wood always addressed the orchestra as a whole when faulty playing occurred. He would never make a man feel small by ticking him off in front of his colleagues but, without looking at the guilty player, he would simply say, 'Gentlemen, let us go back to Section So-and-so'.

Whenever one talks with people who worked in any capacity with Henry Wood, one cannot help being impressed by the fact that the characteristic about him which is always mentioned is his inborn kindness, his affection for his colleagues. One hears over and over again of the singer or instrumentalist who would mention to Wood that he found difficulty in a particular section of his music. 'It *is* difficult', would be the reply. 'You do it very well but if you would like to run through it with me. . . . Don't worry. I shall be with you'. And 'Old Timber' always was there.

As Lady Jessie Wood, who made her Prom début in 1900, told me: 'The truth is that his kindness was the most wonderful thing about him. I never heard him say an unkind thing about anybody. If he was annoyed with somebody, he might murmur, "Oh, he's dotty!" and that was all. Unless something went seriously wrong at a rehearsal, you would never see him ruffled. "It will be all right tonight", he would say. "I'll watch them". His self-confidence was wonderful – completely sure of himself, but in a humble rather than a cocksure way. Even in the war days, you would not hear him grumble about bad playing or indiscipline. It would just be, "Poor darlings. They're all worried". Henry always took care of his singers. So often today a conductor forgets that the singer is a human instrument. Of course, he was a great trainer of an orchestra – but he also trained the public'.

After the morning rehearsal, Wood usually spent the afternoon rehearsing at the piano with the solo singers for that week. And, of course, apart from his Prom commitments, he was in great demand for symphony concerts and as the central figure in music festivals in many parts of the country. Though he did conduct in America, he turned down offers to take over the conductorships of two great American orchestras, the New York Philharmonic and later the Boston Symphony, insisting that his work lay in his own country. In 1921 he was given one of music's most coveted awards, the Gold Medal of the Royal Philharmonic Society, the first British conductor to receive it.

It might well be thought that a man who worked everything out so meticulously by the clock would, when it came to a performance, be a rigid time-beating sort of conductor. But this was not the case and, in fact, the criticism often levelled against him was that he was too much of an 'interpretative' or *rubato* conductor, who stepped between the composer and the audience. This criticism did not worry him in the least. He had no use for the contention about 'letting the music speak for itself', arguing that, unlike the case of a painting, *someone* had to convey the music to the audience and, particularly in a series like the Proms, one of the major aims of which was to attract people to music, it was important to make it as interesting as possible. Left to 'speak for themselves', the dots on the paper would have nothing at all to say. Yet he was ever conscious of his duty to the composer; throughout his life he was constantly re-studying the classics in order to get as close as he could to the composer's intent.

His musical tastes were catholic and he used to insist that he had no favourite pieces. 'I am against the "pet" theory in music,' he would say. He liked jazz – but with reservations : 'I like jazz very much. But for goodness' sake keep it in its place and don't jazz the classics. That is diabolical'.

Wood took the opposite view from Beecham in regard to the inclusion of women players in orchestras. Apart, perhaps, from the harpist, Beecham never employed them. 'If the lady is well-favoured', he said, 'I do not like to play beside her. If she is not, I'm afraid I cannot'. But, as early as 1912, Wood became the first conductor to engage women players in his orchestra, not only as string players but also in the wood-wind department.

As he put it : 'I love to see women in my orchestra. There are some splendid women players. The men are influenced by them, too. A man works in a different way when a girl is working beside him – he cannot slack off.' While he did not think that there should be too big a proportion of women, he contended that every orchestra ought to have its sprinkling of women players. And, of course, when the war came along and many of the men were called into the Forces, he reaped the benefit of his encouragement of the women. In 1935, Marie Wilson became the first woman to lead the orchestra at the Proms, succeeding Charles Wood-house, on his retirement after leading for fifteen years.

Henry Wood made a great number of orchestral arrangements and transcriptions to meet his particular needs in the planning of programmes for the promenade and other concerts he conducted. Two of them won celebrity in quite different ways.

At a Prom in October 1929, an orchestral transcription of Bach's *D Minor Toccata* (the same that Leopold Stokowski arranged for orchestra) was performed. It was described in the programme as by Paul Klenovsky, one of Glazounov's pupils, who had died at an early age. Glazounov, it was stated, had regarded him as one of the greatest masters of orchestration among the young Russian school. The piece went down with great success and was played at subsequent Proms and in many concerts, including those of the Philadelphia Orchestra and at the Hollywood Bowl. It was not until five years after its first performance that the secret of its authorship came out. At that time, it was decided to publish the score, because of its great success. It was true that there had been a Glazounov pupil called Klenovsky but the 'Paul Klenovsky' of the successful transcription was none other than – Henry J Wood. His little joke caused quite a flutter in international musical circles and gave him satisfaction in two ways; he had demonstrated the value attached in this country and elsewhere to a foreign name, and he had got in a sly dig at those critics who had commented adversely on the transcriptions which had appeared under his own name.

Many years earlier, in 1905, there appeared a Henry Wood orchestral arrangement which still holds a prominent place in every Prom season. Robert Newman, with, as usual, a watchful eye on possible topical links, decided to present a concert – not at the Proms – in celebration of the Battle of Trafalgar.

Wood got busy choosing suitably nautical music and, to close the evening, wrote his *Fantasia on British Sea-songs*. It was enthusiastically received and in the following year it was used to wind up the Last Night of the Proms.

It made an enormous impression. When the music reached the 'Hornpipe', the excited Prommers began stamping in time to the music and, entering into the spirit of the evening, Wood pushed the orchestra along faster and faster, while the enthusiastic stampers tried frantically to keep up with him.

The piece was retained in subsequent Prom programmes and, though it was dropped for one season, there was such an outcry from the public that it had to be brought back and has remained to this day a much-loved part of the ebullient ritual of the Last Night of the Proms. Thousands upon thousands of Prommers have taken part in it – and millions of people at home have shared in the excitement by television and radio.

By the time the Proms had been in progress for only a few years, Henry Wood had become a national figure, recognised in the street, written about in the newspapers, and the recipient of a large correspondence – a proportion of it, of course, from crackpots. There was, for instance, the youth who, after intimating that he was anxious to join the Queen's Hall Orchestra, inquired whether they played anything with more sharps than one, as he had so far learned to play only in the key of G. And there was the man who, writing from a north-country town, described himself as a professional and begged advice about improving the tone of his flute-playing—should he wet the instrument or oil it? Unfortunately, Wood's replies to these bizarre requests are not on record.

7

'NO MORE PROMS'

THE PROCESS OF what might be called 'education by enjoyment' proceeded apace. Londoners and visitors to the capital were coming to regard Queen's Hall as a meeting-place with its own special rewards. The 'regulars' no longer came to hear the lighter pieces – which were in any case becoming fewer and were confined to the second half of the programme – but were acquiring a taste for particular composers and, through experience of past pleasant surprises, were ready to explore music by composers of whom they had never, till then, heard. They were becoming accustomed to standing in their own particular spots in the promenade where they were likely to meet their friends. Some of them, well-known figures and ordinary men in the street alike, would just drop in in order to hear a couple of favourite pieces, smoke a cigar or a cigarette, and then pass out again into the London night. Romances were born and hand-holding was not unknown even in those far-off days before the Beatles.

Tchaikovsky and other Russian composers enjoyed great popularity in the early years of the Proms, and this was sometimes built up by careful repetition. In one season, for instance, the *Pathétique* Symphony was played three times and the Fourth and Fifth were each given two performances. Other popular pieces were often played several times in a season as a leaven for the less familiar offerings. Such works as Wagner's *Tannhäuser* Overture or Grieg's *Peer Gynt* Suite might be played four or five times in the same season.

The generous sound of Wagner caught on from the start but Beethoven was not an immediate box-office draw. It took several years of Friday nights, giving all the nine symphonies and all the concertos, before audiences came along in strength.

But Wood realised that the 'educational' side of the Proms must not be overdone. 'You cannot force Bach and Beethoven down people's throats', he said. 'Give it them in small doses at first and perhaps they will learn to love it and ask for more.' And indeed they did.

By the nineteen-twenties he was able to say, proudly, that the best houses of the season had been for the classical programmes and that Bach had really come into his own at the Proms.

'I think a lot of it has to do with the kind of performance when we do Bach', he said, 'We now put a little more expression into his wonderfully moving melodies. When I was a boy they used to make them stodgy and I think that made the public fight shy of Bach.'

A typical week's Proms in 1930 looked something like this : Monday – Wagner Night; Tuesday – Miscellaneous, including popular symphonies; Wednesday – Bach alternating with Brahms; Thursday – British composers; Friday – Beethoven; Saturday – Miscellaneous popular night.

While giving an ever fuller classical representation, Sir Henry was able to look back upon the great number

of important works he had introduced to London and,
in many cases, to England. In the very early years of
the Proms, for instance, he had given first performances
here of such works as:

Rimsky-Korsakov's *Capriccio Espagnol* and Symphony
No 2 (*Antar*)
Tchaikovsky's first three symphonies, the *Manfred*
Symphony, and the *Casse-Noisette* and *Swan Lake*
Suites
Rachmaninov's First Piano Concerto
Elgar's *Pomp and Circumstance* March No 1, with its
'Land of Hope and Glory' section in the middle (they
had to play this march three times)
Glazounov's *The Seasons*
Sibelius's First Symphony and *The Swan of Tuonela*
Mahler's First and Fourth Symphonies
Debussy's *L'Après-midi d'une faune.*
It was a remarkable record and the work of
cunningly combining novelties with standard fare
went steadily on.

Richard Strauss's music, which was given a good
showing in the programmes, was slow to gain favour
with Prom audiences; but perseverance brought its
rewards and it gradually made its mark.
The Queen's Hall Proms took a tip from the Crystal
Palace concerts of August Manns in providing informa-
tive programme notes from the start. One of the most
distinguished writers of these was Mrs Rosa Newmarch,
who was the official annotator from 1908 until 1920.
She was an authority on Russian and Slav music in
particular and a devoted admirer of Henry Wood, to

whom she dedicated the six volumes of her programme notes with the words: 'To Sir Henry J Wood, the motive power which kept us all moving forward – From the Fly-on-the-Wheel'.

Some of the more popular items in the Prom programmes became something of an embarrassment because of the audience's clamour for encores and eventually it had to be insisted that there could be no encores in the first halves of programmes.

At quite an early stage the experiment was tried of presenting series of Winter Proms but—as happened again much more recently—they never captured the public's fancy to anything like the extent of those earlier in the year. The question still remains: Where do the Prommers go in the winter-time?

In terms of artistry and popularity, the Proms were a success, but it would have been surprising if their progress through the years had been free from setbacks. There were to be many crises before they achieved the secure financial backing they enjoy today.

The programme build-up proceeded steadily and the concerts were in the main satisfactorily attended but, although the costs of concert promotion were only a fraction of the immense expense involved in running a symphony orchestra today, the financial burden was nevertheless heavy in relation to the conditions of the time. There was no such thing as a state or municipal grant for the Proms. The financial side presented a problem for individuals to solve as best they could.

It proved too much for Robert Newman, experienced business man though he was, and – through other promotions, one gathers, rather than simply through the Proms – he went bankrupt in 1902. Here was crisis indeed, but, as was to happen again in subsequent crises, there was someone who appreciated the value of the Proms and was not only willing but also able to help.

The man who came to the rescue in this first crisis was Edgar (later Sir Edgar) Speyer, a German-born financier who had taken over the direction of the London end of the family interests and had become a naturalised British subject. Apart from being a lover of music, Speyer had a personal link with the Queen's Hall concerts through his American-born wife, Leonora von Stosch, who had made several successful Prom appearances as a solo violinist.

Speyer formed a syndicate which undertook the financial side of running the Proms, Robert Newman remaining as manager and secretary of the orchestra, the first title of which had been 'Robert Newman's Queen's Hall Orchestra'. It now became simply 'The Queen's Hall Orchestra' and, still of course under the direction of Henry Wood, it carried on the Proms.

The second crisis was an artistic rather than a financial one, though it did hinge on the personal finances of members of the Queen's Hall Orchestra. It was the row over the 'deputies system' and it blew up in 1904. Among orchestral players at this time it was the recognised thing that a player might send along a deputy to represent him at a rehearsal or a concert. Thus, a conductor might spend a heavy morning in rehearsal, only to find that, when he walked on to the platform for the evening's concert, there were in the orchestra several strange faces, none of whose owners had rehearsed the programme with him.

77

The story goes that one conductor at this time had been fortunate enough to have several rehearsals for a London concert but had noticed changes in the personnel of the orchestra. At the final rehearsal, however, he was gratified to see that one player, at any rate, had always been present. The conductor thanked him for the high standard of his playing and for his diligent attendance at rehearsal and said that he looked forward to seeing him in the evening. 'Oh', said the player, 'I shan't be here tonight – I'm sending a deputy'.

Henry Wood suffered a good deal under this system, whereby a player could absent himself if a more lucrative engagement turned up, but he and Robert Newman were not the sort of men to allow their efforts at achieving high standards to be frustrated in this way. They decided that the impossible situation must be brought to an end. Newman announced brusquely to the orchestra that in future there would be no more deputies – and the storm broke.

The orchestra met to discuss the position and about half of them decided to resign, leaving Newman and Wood to recruit other players on their new terms. But that was not the end of the 'rebels'. They formed their own orchestra on a self-governing basis, and called it the London Symphony Orchestra, the original of the splended LSO of today. So that, with the Queen's Hall Orchestra building up again, there were now two fine orchestras in London – and both of them largely trained by Henry Wood!

The outbreak of World War I brought several problems – and another major crisis – for the Proms. There were the difficulties of the sort suffered by the country in general under wartime conditions. Some members of the orchestra left to join the Forces and now Henry Wood's enterprise of two years earlier in encouraging women to make a career of orchestral playing brought its rewards. The gaps in the ranks were filled without great difficulty.

But the war brought with it a violent upsurge in anti-German feeling, immediately reflected in the disappearance of the Monday night Wagner programme which had become one of the most popular features of the Proms. Those who had enjoyed these programmes through the years strongly objected to the view that, because Britain was at war with Germany, there should be an end to the performance of the music of a great German composer at the Proms. Henry Wood and Robert Newman were at pains to make it clear that they were not responsible for the change and a slip of paper, setting out the position, was inserted in the Prom programme :

> The Directors of the Queen's Hall Orchestra think that some explanation of the change of programme on Monday evening, August 17, is due to their Subscribers and to all who have so loyally supported the Promenade Concerts in the past.
>
> The substitution of a mixed programme in place of a wholly Wagnerian one was not dictated by any narrow-minded intolerant policy, but was the result of outside pressure brought to bear upon the Lessees of the Queen's Hall.
>
> With regard to the future, the Directors hope – with the broadminded co-operation of their audience – to carry through as nearly as possible the original scheme of the Concerts as set forth in the Prospectus. They take the opportunity of emphatically contradicting the statements that German music will be

boycotted during the present season. The greatest examples of Music and Art are world possessions and unassailable even by the prejudices and passions of the hour.

But the war did have its reflection in the Prom programmes by the inclusion of the National Anthems of the Allies. As, however, more and more countries joined the Allied cause, the number of anthems to be played became embarrassingly large, and a compromise was reached by spreading them over different nights, otherwise Prom audiences might have found themselves listening to programmes that consisted almost entirely of the National Anthems of the Allies!

Crisis came again on the financial side of the running of the Proms when Sir Edgar Speyer decided to withdraw and to leave the country for America. Speyer was a man of culture who had played a prominent part in the life of this country. His firm had been interested in many important undertakings, including the London underground railways. He was one of the founders of the Whitechapel Art Gallery; he was created a baronet in 1906 and a Privy Councillor three years later. Yet, three years after the war had ended, his name was to be brought up before the Certificates of Naturalisation (Revocation) Committee, set up under an act of 1914. As a result he was denaturalised and removed from membership of the Privy Council on the ground of disloyalty to the King and unlawful communication with the enemy. Be that as it may, his support of the Proms over a long period had brought highly satisfactory results, and is said to have cost him about £30,000.

Again the Proms were left without financial backing.

This time it was the music-publishing firm of Chappell who stepped in to the rescue, after having been lessees of Queen's Hall for some years. And again the orchestra acquired another name: 'The New Queen's Hall Orchestra'.

The new arrangement worked very well indeed until another double blow was struck at the Proms. First of all, Robert Newman died in 1926 at the age of sixty-six.

Wood and Newman were men of quite different temperaments but each was fully appreciative of the other's particular abilities and together they made a great working team. Wood was devoted to Newman and, especially in the earliest days of the Proms, could not have done without him. By the time of Newman's death, however, it would seem that Wood, artistically equipped from the start, had also acquired the necessary knowledge of the running of the business side of the concerts.

But then, soon after Newman's death, came the greatest crisis in the story of the Proms. Messrs Chappell decided that they could no longer shoulder the financial burden and this time it really looked as though the Proms would have to come to an end.

Only a year earlier, the then Dr Adrian Boult, musical director of Birmingham City Orchestra, had summed up the achievement of the Proms:

> I have often said (and I have never been contra-dicted) that in my opinion the average standard of performance throughout the promenade season is higher under Sir Henry Wood's direction than could be possible under any other living conductor. The worst performance one could ever hear at the

promenade concerts would do credit to many well-known concert-giving institutions, and the best will bear comparison with anything to be heard throughout the world.

And now it seemed that all was over. So firmly established had the Proms become in the life of the country that the news of their threatened end created a sensation. The newspaper placards read: 'NO MORE PROMS'. People in the audience at concerts conducted by Sir Henry Wood and those who saw him in the street greeted him with greater warmth than ever and shouted: 'We won't let you go'. There was no doubt about the genuineness of the dismay that the news had caused. But, apart from the warmth of sentiment, what was to be done about it in a practical way?

In a leading article in March 1927, *The Times* summed up the gravity of the situation, expressing the general dismay of all who had learnt to think of Sir Henry Wood and his orchestra as the one constant factor in the musical life of London:

> For thirty-three years Londoners kept at work during August and September have consoled themselves with the 'Promenades'. Some have even preferred to take their holidays early or late so as not to miss their annual chance of hearing Beethoven's symphonies, or the best of Wagner, or whatever their special taste in music might be.
>
> The suggestion that there will be no more 'Promenades' is likely to be received at first with incredulity, as a mere scare, because they have been so long in the reckoning, and the next tendency will be to blame somebody for the withdrawal of one of the amenities of London life. It should be said at once that there is no room either for doubt or for blame.

The paper pointed out that for many years Messrs
Chappell had financed the New Queen's Hall
Orchestra, rarely making, and often losing, money
over the season. They did not wish to incur further
risks and had no obligation to do so.

After commenting upon the services of the Proms to
young artists and composers, *The Times* pointed out:
'Musicians of other countries have begun to see in the
Queen's Hall Promenade season a sort of trying-ground
where what is new and good of both native and foreign
music may be discovered. The scheme of programmes
is carefully watched on the other side of the Atlantic,
and programme-makers there are not above taking a
hint'.

While contending that there must be some people
in London who could afford to spend a comparatively
small sum in maintaining an institution so manifestly
for the public good, the article added: 'It is no use
supposing that the concerts can be made to pay as a
commercial project, and it would be better that they
should cease now, and Sir Henry Wood allowed to go
to the artistic work which invites him elsewhere, than
that they should be dragged on with the necessary
lowering of standard which a purely commercial
management entails'.

Though bitterly distressed and disappointed at the
turn that events had taken, Sir Henry Wood faced the
situation realistically: 'I am, of course, the greatest
admirer of what Messrs Chappell have done. The
scheme has not been a financial success so far as they
are concerned. They have seen us through, and all we
musicians, orchestral players and artists, are very
grateful to them. They have carried on for years and

must have lost something like £60,000 in the interests of the musical public of London and of England. But they do not see the commercial value of running the Queen's Hall Orchestra any longer.

'I think I am right in saying we have done more to encourage British artists than any other organisation. We employ young people and encourage young artists, and the ''Promenades'' have such world-wide fame that it would be a very serious thing for our reputation on the Continent if they ceased. It would indeed give them an opportunity to call us unmusical.

'It would be a disgrace to this country if the ''Promenades'' were to go. But we have done so much that I am sure that we are going to do a great deal more. The education that has been given to the public is going to tell, and the help given by broadcasting and by very fine gramophone records is, I am sure, going to bear very great fruit in the future'.

In *Punch* there appeared a cartoon which, recalling the generosity of London's Philharmonic Society to Beethoven at a time of need, depicted Sir Henry Wood walking away from Queen's Hall with a bundle of scores under his arm and in the distance the newspaper placard: 'NO MORE PROMS'. Behind him walked the shade of Beethoven, saying: 'This is indeed tragic, but I cannot believe that this rich city, once so generous to me, will fail to find us a permanent home'.

At this time, broadcasting was a comparatively new medium and its development was watched with grave concern by concert promoters who feared that, with music being poured directly into every home, they might be put out of business. The same fears possessed the gramophone industry, which, when one looks at the situation today, can hardly be said to have been damaged by broadcasting!

Yet, somewhat ironically, it was broadcasting which saved the Proms. In June 1927, the BBC made this announcement, just when hopes of a solution were fading:

'Ever since the possible suspension of the Queen's Hall Promenades was announced, the Corporation has been anxious to do whatever was in its power, consistent with its wider obligations, to bring about an arrangement not only with regard to the Promenades, but also on the larger issue of Queen's Hall.

'Negotiations have been in progress for several months. A number of proposals have been considered and abandoned. Ultimately, however, agreement has been reached between the BBC and Messrs Chappell. A six-weeks' series of Promenade Concerts at the Queen's Hall, starting on Saturday, August 13, is to be given by the BBC under the conductorship of Sir Henry Wood.

'The BBC is also to give twelve special Symphony Concerts at the Queen's Hall during next season. Moreover, the microphone is no longer banned from the Queen's Hall for other occasions.'

The clouds which had gathered over the Proms had been dispersed.

8

BASIL CAMERON — AND
PROMS IMPROMPTU

UNDER THE NEW BBC régime, Sir Henry Wood
enjoyed several advantages over the old days,
notably the greatly increased facilities for rehearsal of
his concerts. Those three three-hour rehearsals for the
six concerts in the week had imposed a heavy strain;
now he was able to devote more time to the works
which called for fuller preparation. It was no longer
necessary to repeat a work several times in the season.

With the rigid timing of broadcast programmes,
encores, which had already been restricted to the
second half of the programme, were now cut out
altogether, much to the satisfaction of Sir Henry, who
had never relished these breaks in the continuity of
the programmes as planned. And, while retaining the
intimacy of his audience of about 2,500 in a full
Queen's Hall, he now embraced also the great radio
audience. The title of the orchestra underwent further
changes – 'Sir Henry Wood and His Symphony
Orchestra,' and later, when the BBC created their fine
new orchestra in 1930, 'Sir Henry Wood and the
BBC Symphony Orchestra'.

Apart from himself, he still had a personal link
with the days of Robert Newman in W W Thompson,

who had become Newman's assistant as a very young man and now managed the Proms. He was to be concerts manager of the BBC for a long period up to his retirement a few years ago.

Many Prom traditions were firmly established. In the 'Gluepot' round the corner business flourished, and a large hand-bell was brought into action to signal to members of the orchestra and the audience that the interval had come to an end and it was time to return to Queen's Hall. On Last Nights there was the ever-quickening stamping to the hornpipe in the *Sea Songs*, and there was Sir Henry's own little bit of pantomime in which he indicated that the evening had really come to a close by walking on to the platform wearing his overcoat and carrying his hat in his hand. Sometimes he teased his audience by coming on at first with a borrowed coat over his arm, to be followed later by the wearing of his own coat. Then it really was time for everybody to go home.

The 1939 season opened on 12th August, with the shadows of impending war darkening over the world, and came to a premature close on 1st September. To ensure the continuance of the broadcasting service, the BBC's various departments, including the symphony orchestra, were dispersed to different parts of the country and, when 1940 arrived, it seemed that there would be no Proms at Queen's Hall. But Mr Keith Douglas, honorary secretary of the Royal Philharmonic Society, with Mr Owen Mase, decided to continue the concerts under the auspices of the RPS. And – a nicely ironic touch – the orchestra they engaged was the London Symphony, the orchestra that had come into existence as a result of the 'rebellion' over the deputies system all those years earlier. It was the 'rebel orchestra', though not of course the same individuals, that kept the Proms going!

For the first time in the history of the Proms, Sir Henry Wood, now seventy-one, had with him an associate conductor to share the burden of the season, and the choice fell upon Basil Cameron – who was to be the central figure in the strangest of all promenade concerts. 'A born conductor', Sir Henry called him.

Mr Cameron was no 'new boy' at the Proms, having been a violinist in the Queen's Hall Orchestra as a youngster before going on to a distinguished career as a conductor, a career which started perhaps rather inauspiciously with being sacked from his church choir and receiving a hearty clout over the head from his violin teacher!

He was born in Reading, the son of a church organist, and it was while the family were living in Tiverton, in Devon, that the seven-year-old Basil was a member of the church choir.

'But', he told me, 'after choir practice one evening, the curate came out and found me playing leapfrog over the tombstones. I was promptly asked to leave the choir.

'My father taught me the piano and when I was about seven I was having violin lessons from Otto Milani in Tiverton. I had the cheek of the devil – no nerves at all.

'I made my first public appearance at the age of eight, rattling off a concerto in a concert at Exeter. In the same concert, a girl played the Mendelssohn concerto and, when I was introduced to her afterwards, I said, "I did enjoy your playing. You play much better than Mr Milani". For which Mr Milani clouted my ears when I went for my next lesson.'

But at the age of fourteen he was leading an orchestra in Scarborough at two pounds five shillings a week – 'good money then'. After study with Joachim in Berlin – 'he was a terrifying old boy' – he joined the Queen's Hall Orchestra in 1908 and stayed for five seasons.

'I learned more about conducting from Henry Wood than from anybody else', said Mr Cameron. 'He was so very thorough and he had a wonderful stick-technique.

'After leaving Queen's Hall I took over the municipal orchestra at Torquay – Henry Wood recommended me for it – and in my first year I put on a Wagner Festival to celebrate the centenary of the composer's birth, getting down half the Queen's Hall Orchestra to augment my little orchestra. The festival created quite a stir. Bernard Shaw came down to hear us and became quite a fan of mine!

'Of course, when I was a violinist in the Queen's Hall Orchestra I was much too small fry to know the great Robert Newman. But I did have a feeling of satisfaction years later when I was back in London and looked in at a rehearsal at Queen's Hall. Newman came over and said that they were losing their timpanist and could I recommend a man who had worked with me in Torquay. I felt quite important!'

Fritz Kreisler was a friend of Basil Cameron – 'I always think of him as an example of the hard work that a great artist puts into his job. I have heard him in his hotel room, going over and over a phrase of a few notes for half an hour, just to get it as he wanted it.'

Sibelius, too, became a friend whom he visited many times at his home in Helsinki. If that much-talked-of Eighth Symphony had ever seen the light of day, it would probably have been given its first performance in this country by Basil Cameron. One of his treasured possessions is a letter in which the great Finnish composer wrote, 'My Eighth Symphony has been "finished" many times but I am not contented with it. When the time comes it will be a pleasure to me to give it in your hands.' Sibelius died and the symphony never was finished to his satisfaction.

Cameron spent two seasons with the San Francisco Symphony Orchestra, sharing the conducting with Issay Dobrowen, and then six years with the Seattle Symphony Orchestra before coming back to London to assist Sir Thomas Beecham at Covent Garden. On one night, because Beecham had contracted a chill, he conducted a performance of *Tristan und Isolde* at very short notice and without a full rehearsal.

It will be seen therefore that, in picking Basil Cameron as the first associate conductor in the history of the Proms, Sir Henry Wood chose a gifted musician of all-round experience, a highly professional conductor of the no-nonsense sort, as well as a man for whom he had warm personal regard.

It was a most satisfactory set-up but the 1940 Proms had not been long in progress before that fervent Wagnerian, Adolf Hitler, decided to add his own percussive embellishments to the proceedings in Queen's Hall. He opened up his blitz on London; and it was a shining example of the way in which people hunger for the decent things in life that the Proms went on while all hell was let loose outside

Queen's Hall. The Proms, still performing their proper proportion of great German music, were never more popular than when they were competing with Hitler's particular form of culture.

In retrospect, the 1940 Proms become more and more fantastic. Night after night the German bombers came over, relieving themselves of their loads of high explosives and incendiaries – you could almost set your watch by the time the uproar started – and night after night the queues formed in Langham Place, queues of hundreds of people seeking refreshment and solace in the midst of the horror. One bomb on Queen's Hall would have caused a shambles, but the undaunted Prommers continued to line up as early as five o'clock in the evening.

Within the hall there was a system of warning notices and of coloured lights indicating that an 'Alert' had been sounded or that a raid was imminent. The audience stayed and the concert proceeded. And at the end of the advertised programme it was announced that those who wished to remain instead of going out into the streets could do so. It was then that the impromptu Proms began. The audience did stay – sometimes until five o'clock in the morning – and so did the London Symphony Orchestra.

Basil Cameron presided over the extraordinary proceedings. There would be community singing, with that great and 'unashamed' accompanist, Gerald Moore, sitting at the piano and revealing that he knew every song that might be asked for. Instrumentalists, glad to step out from the comparative anonymity of the orchestra, emerged as brilliant soloists.

Basil Cameron recalls : 'I remember a young woman violinist was playing a most intricate concerto when the red light went on – almost at the end of her bow. She carried on, quite unshaken. We had some splendid concerts after the original concert finished. Chaps in the orchestra would offer to play, say, a bassoon solo or a 'cello solo and we just carried on.

'The audience thoroughly enjoyed themselves and did not want to go home. One night Sir Adrian Boult strolled in just when we were going to do the *Toy Symphony*. He joined in on the triangle. And Benno Moiseiwitsch, who had been the soloist in the evening's concert, stayed on and played the piano part in Schubert's *Trout* quintet, which he had never played before. We just stuck the music in front of him.

'One of the great moments was when we announced that a famous conductor "now in Australia" would conduct the *Figaro* overture. On to the platform walked Sir Thomas Beecham – or the exact image of him – and proceeded to conduct the overture with all the typical mannerisms. He was given a tremendous reception. He was, in fact, Ralph Nicholson, a violinist in the LSO, who now teaches at one of the colleges in London.'

On some nights, after the professionals had performed, members of the audience would seize the chance of showing off their talents in Queen's Hall. A young man in his late 'teens received an ovation for his playing of some piano pieces by Debussy, an Indian sang unaccompanied love-songs of his native land, and – particularly impressive in view of the Hitler-inspired din going on outside – a young girl sang German lieder.

93

There would be coffee and sandwiches, and audience and orchestra would eventually disperse, some to face their day's work in the office and some to prepare for rehearsal of the next evening's concert. So popular were these impromptu Proms that, so it is said, a woman put her head in at the box-office one morning and asked the manager if there was going to be a raid that evening. Understandably, he said that he really had no idea. 'Oh', said the woman, 'I was coming to the concert only if there was going to be a raid.'

Eventually, however, with the intensifying of the air raids, the authorities decided that the time had come to call a halt. The last Prom at Queen's Hall was presented on 7th September 1940; and, true to the tradition, it contained a 'novelty', the first performance of *Three Pieces for Orchestra* by the British composer Elizabeth Lutyens. This was the programme:

Variations on 'Three Blind Mice'	Holbrooke
Bell Song from *Lakmé*	Delibes
Joan Tribe	
Piano Concerto No 2	Rachmaninov
Benno Moiseiwitsch	
En Saga	Sibelius
'E lucevan le stelle' from *Tosca*	Puccini
Frank Titterton	
Three Pieces for Orchestra	Lutyens
Three Slavonic Dances	Dvorak
London Pageant	Bax
Ruy Blas Overture	Mendelssohn

That was the end of the Proms at Queen's Hall but it was not the last concert. In May 1941 Malcolm Sargent conducted the Royal Choral Society and the

London Philharmonic Orchestra in an afternoon performance of Elgar's *The Dream of Gerontius*, with Muriel Brunskill, Webster Booth and Ronald Stear as soloists. That night, three hundred German bombers struck at London, causing widespread damage and casualties. Incendiary bombs fell on Queen's Hall and, hampered by breakdowns in the water-supply, the fire-fighters were helpless to stem the flames. All that was left was the battered shell of London's much-loved concert hall.

In the years after the war, various schemes were put forward for the building of a new hall on the same site but all of them came to naught.

Where Queen's Hall used to be, there now stands the St George's Hotel. But if you walk down Great Portland Street and look along a narrow lane at the back of the hotel that used to be the nearest exit for the 'Gluepot', you can still just make out, at the top of a low wall, the letters, Q-U-E-E-N-S H-A-L-L.

9

OUR FRIEND ALBERT

WHILE SIR THOMAS Beecham was rehearsing his orchestra for a concert in the Royal Albert Hall, there came the sound of violent and persistent hammering from without.

'Splendid!' exclaimed Sir Thomas, enthusiastically. 'They're knocking the damn place down at last.'

Poor old Albert Hall. There surely cannot be any London edifice – unless it be the Albert Memorial, its neighbour over the road – that has come in for more banter and ridicule. For years it has been regarded as fair game for those who are obsessed by the fussiness of the Victorian age and forget its greatness.

Beecham, of course – being, not a Victorian, but an Elizabethan character born in the reign of Victoria – had plenty to say about it. 'The Royal Albert Hall', he remarked, 'has much to say for itself in the field of low comedy. But it is invaluable for those who are slow on the musical uptake – they hear everything three times. And it is the only place in which some composers are likely to hear more than one performance of their works.'

The Albert Hall and its echo. . . .

Leopold Stokowski put it rather more kindly than Beecham. 'You know', he said to me after he had been rehearsing there, 'if Albert Hall would lend a few resonances to Festival Hall, you would have two fine concert halls.'

But, with all the standard jokes about the Albert Hall, there are many of us who confess to an affection for the old place, despite its comicalities – perhaps even because of some of them. One of the great features about the Albert Hall is that it never seems to be surprised at anything. The product of a great age, it has a serenity about it and in its vast capacity it cheerfully embraces whatever may come along. In 1971 it celebrates the centenary of its opening by Queen Victoria, and through the years it has seen most things.

Its conception and building were full of frustrations and involvements. It was built on the Kensington site of Gore House, where one of the last residents was a French gentleman who established, of all things, a 'Vatican of Gastronomy', where he successfully cashed in upon the hunger of visitors to the Great Exhibition of 1851.

It was out of the profits from the Exhibition that the Royal Commissioners embarked on a project for a great centre for arts and sciences, embracing the plan for a magnificent hall. The building site was leased for 999 years at a rental of one shilling a year. What kind of music will be heard in the Royal Albert Hall by the time the lease runs out is anybody's conjecture.

The foundation stone was laid in 1867 and, after many complications and setbacks, the building was completed and, amid tremendous ceremony, was officially opened by Queen Victoria four years later.

If you take a seat for the Proms at the back of the stalls you may find yourself almost leaning against

the foundation stone. It is fixed just behind the gang-
way seats K1083 and K1083A and is built into the
front of the loggia. You have to crouch down to see it
and you may well think that this is an odd place in
which to put a foundation stone. But you must
remember that you are in the Royal Albert Hall.

You may think it strange, too, to hear that a concert
is 'sold out' and yet to find that there are empty seats
on the night. Here you encounter one of the unique
features about the running of the Albert Hall. This is
how it is explained by Mr F J Mundy, the manager,
whose predecessors have included Charles Taylor,
one-time manager of Queen's Hall, and Sir Charles
Cochran:

'It goes back to the origins of the hall. When it was
being built, they ran short of money and hit on the
idea of selling seats to private holders at £100 a time
for 999 years, with the right to bequeath them or sell
them. At first they were entitled to their seats for
everything that happened in the Albert Hall. But
there have been changes since then and seat-holders
have had to pay an annual sum towards the amenities
of the hall and they may also be excluded from not
more than twelve events – concerts, boxing, or
wrestling – in the year.

'There are at present 1287 seats held by 350 people
or firms. On a full night at the Proms there are 4900
people sitting down, 1250 standing in the arena and
1150 sitting on the floor in the gallery.'

The Queen owns twenty seats in the grand tier,
which were bought for £2000 by Queen Victoria and
which constitute the 'Queen's Box', formerly called
the 'Royal Box'. But, when the Queen is not there,

the seats do not remain empty. By her permission, members of the Royal household are allowed to use them or sometimes such an organisation as the Victoria League is asked to invite overseas visitors to enjoy the thrill of listening to a concert from the 'Queen's Box'.

On one occasion, when the special floor was being laid down for a gala ball and some of the seats were put out of commission, two women seat-holders insisted upon having a hole cut in the floor so that the seats could be used. Whether or not they enjoyed the proceedings is not recorded but at any rate they stood upon – or rather sat upon – their rights.

Again, you may have wondered about the courteous gentlemen who show you to your place in the hall and seem familiar with all the ins and outs of the place. Their function, too, goes back to the earliest days of the hall. There were volunteer stewards at the opening ceremony and later the Corps of Honorary Stewards was formed.

'There are about eighty of them today and they are extremely loyal and valuable', says Mr Mundy. 'They do this work because they love the Albert Hall. They all give their services without payment and they have to undertake to work on at least half of the events in the year. We pay their travelling expenses and they receive two tickets for each show at which they officiate.'

One of the stewards, by the way, was involved in a quaint incident when the Philharmonia were giving a concert in the Albert Hall a few years ago. For the performance of Beethoven's *Leonora No 3* overture, trumpeter Elgar Howarth was stationed in the corridor up in the heights in order to play the distant trumpet calls. But no sooner had he raised his trumpet to his lips than, still sturdily blowing, he was seized by an alert steward and – with a 'You can't do that there 'ere', but in politer language, of course – was propelled into the bar, where he was able to explain the situation in time to return for his second trumpet-call. The steward was, of course, quite right. Nobody had told him and, dash it, you can't have people blowing trumpets all over the place when there is a concert going on!

As every Prommer knows, the Albert Hall, when full, presents an exciting spectacle, with the crowd in the arena, the rising tiers of seats, and, although you can hardly see them from below, the other Prommers who are sitting on the floor up in the gallery.

They are the people who do not particularly want to see what goes on, except perhaps in a bird's eye sort of way, but who really do want to hear. The sound up there is excellent. They have been joined from time to time in the past by Sir Adrian Boult, who has called in to listen to a performance in which he has had special interest. In studying his own scores at home, Sir Adrian's favourite posture used to be achieved by stretching his considerable length on the floor. It cannot be said that he has been observed lying flat on his face in the gallery of the Royal Abert Hall, but he has certainly been there on many occasions, the diligent listener.

The Albert Hall empty – a splendid place to get lost in among its corridors and staircases – is richly evocative. The ghosts walk.

Many distinguished artists have been shaken when

101

they first looked out upon the vastness of the place. Wagner certainly was. Queen Victoria found herself overcome by emotion and unable to pronounce the words declaring the hall open; but in her case this was surely not because the great Queen was overawed by the Royal Albert Hall, but because it had grown out of the dream of her beloved Consort who had died ten years earlier. To her it was Albert's Hall. The Prince of Wales, later Edward VII, stepped in and spoke the official words of opening for her.

Walk the corridors of the Albert Hall and the shade of Adelina Patti, a great favourite there, brushes by. Charles Gounod will be around, rather disgruntled because they did not care for his choice of music as the first conductor of what was to become the Royal Choral Society. And you might encounter Wagner, who took part in the conducting of a festival of his music, or Verdi, who conducted the first London performance of his great *Requiem* in the hall where we now hear the Proms. Chaliapin, McCormack, Gigli – the much-loved voices linger on – and you may be sure that, away up in the heights, the closing words of 'Land of Hope and Glory' are still resounding in the massive tones of Dame Clara Butt. It is not every artist whose voice projects satisfactorily in the Royal Albert Hall. Clara Butt's not only did but must have seriously endangered the security of the place; it was not necessarily everybody's favourite sound, but a sound not to be ignored.

There have been the great national rallies, the high jinks of the suffragettes, cycling events, wrestling, the pageantry of *Hiawatha*, and, though not until after much heated discussion, boxing. The designers of the

102

hall had in mind the Colosseum of Rome and today, when the Proms are not in possession, you may enjoy the spectacle of modern gladiators hammering out of each other such sense as they possess. But you will not see anyone being thrown to the lions. Lions are out. The Charter does not permit live animals or birds to be taken into the building. *Le Carnaval des Animaux*, *Ma Mère l'Oye*, and *Peter and the Wolf* are, however, quite all right.

The Royal Albert Hall had seen and heard almost everything and, when Queen's Hall was destroyed, was calmly waiting to be of service, a little scarred but unshaken.

Not by any means everyone was enthusiastic about the idea of taking the Proms to the Albert Hall. Queen's Hall, on a full night, had comfortably accommodated some 2500 people in a pleasantly intimate atmosphere, but in the Albert Hall, with its space for about 6000, would not the Prom audience look lost? And surely that 'family gathering' feeling, which had been so much a characteristic of the Proms, was bound to disappear? There was, too, that old question of acoustics.

Mr Keith Douglas, however, displayed the determination and the optimism of a Yorkshireman and decided to go ahead with a 1941 season of six weeks under the auspices of the Royal Philharmonic Society. He again engaged the London Symphony Orchestra, with Sir Henry Wood as conductor and Basil Cameron as his associate, and, in order to give audiences a chance to get home before the full wartime black-out descended on London, the concerts were timed to begin at 6.30 pm and to end at nine o'clock at the latest. In the programmes was this note : 'In the event of an air-raid warning the audience is requested to leave the auditorium immediately and carry out the instructions of the stewards and attendants. Shelter is provided in the various corridors, but if any person should wish to leave the building the nearest public shelters are : Trenches in Kensington Gardens. Trenches in Hyde Park. Subway in Exhibition Road.'

But first of all Mr Douglas set himself to see what could be done about the acoustics of the Albert Hall. In the years since the hall was opened there had often been discussions on acoustical matters and various steps had been taken. Indeed, Ronald W Clark records, in his exhaustive book *The Royal Albert Hall*,[1] that in the 1930's, the resonances had been studied during the playing of the organ and the suggestion had seriously been made that perhaps the shingled hair and short skirts of the ladies in the audience had been absorbing less sound than the long hair and fuller dresses of the Edwardians. Perhaps there is an interesting treatise yet to be written on the effect of the mini-skirt upon the acoustics at the Proms!

Before the season opened it was decided to lower the 'velarium' – the massive sheet of linen designed to catch anything which might fall from the roof, and modelled on the arrangement in the old Roman amphitheatres to protect the spectators from the rain. Later, however, the authorities ruled that the velarium must be raised again, as any splinters of glass from above might gain enough impetus to cut through. However, a system of screens in the vicinity of the

---

[1] *The Royal Albert Hall*, Ronald W Clark, Hamish Hamilton.

orchestra had beneficial effects on the quality of the sound.

What is seen high up near the roof nowadays, by the way, is not the velarium but a later addition, a huge metal canopy which has the appearance of being fluted but which is in fact an arrangement of metal cylinders packed with wire wool.

As to the audience, a sort of 'Parkinson's Law' came into operation and, instead of the Queen's Hall-size audience being lost in the Albert Hall, the greater space attracted more people. True, the 'regulars' understandably bemoaned the loss of their old surroundings, but a good deal of the spirit of the Proms was successfully carried over to the new setting.

During that season the programmes included a Dvorak Centenary Concert, starting with the Czech National Anthem – particularly poignant at that time – and an Anglo-American Concert, in which works by three distinguished American composers, Samuel Barber, John Alden Carpenter, and Ernest Schelling, were included.

The BBC took up the running of the Proms again in 1942 and, to ease the strain on conductors and players, they employed two orchestras, their own Symphony Orchestra and the London Philharmonic, and three conductors, Sir Henry Wood and two associates, Basil Cameron and Sir Adrian Boult. And they announced that, though anyone in the audience could leave in the event of an air-raid warning, the concerts would continue.

It was during this season that Sir Henry Wood gave the first performance in this country of Shostakovich's Seventh Symphony, dubbed the *Leningrad Symphony* because it was composed in tribute to the spirit of the besieged city, where part of it was composed. A special plane flew the orchestral parts to England but when they arrived Wood found that the copyists had made a number of mistakes. With the aid of the diligent Gustave de Mauney, he set about making the corrections, starting at eight o'clock in the morning and completing the job six days later, working on the tops of a couple of packing-cases while his furniture was being moved to a new flat. It was this symphony which first brought Shostakovich's name before most people in this country.

Benjamin Britten's *Sinfonia da Requiem* and Aaron Copland's ballet suite, *Billy the Kid*, had their first British performances and there were premières of Moeran's Violin Concerto and Rubbra's Fourth Symphony.

Though Sir Adrian Boult did not conduct at the Proms until 1942, his behind-the-scenes influence had already been strongly felt. For the BBC Symphony Orchestra became – and still is – the backbone of the Proms, and Sir Adrian was its architect, an apt description of a man who has always had a keen sense of the form and structure of music. He had been conductor of the City of Birmingham Symphony Orchestra for six years when, in 1930, he joined the BBC as musical director and conductor of the Symphony Orchestra which was just being formed on a permanent basis. Many of the finest players in the country – 120-strong in the original form – were brought together and Sir Adrian proceeded to weld his forces into one of the finest orchestral instruments in the world.

I recall that when Colin Davis was about to take up his appointment as principal conductor of the BBC Symphony Orchestra he said to me: 'When I was very young I used to listen a great deal to Sir Ardian Boult's broadcasts. I felt that he was laying the classics clearly before me – that this was what they were about. I shall always be grateful to him for that.'

It seems that Mr Davis got the message. Sir Adrian's purpose has always been to get as close as possible to the composer's intent rather than to stand between the composer and the listener. Like Henry Wood before him, he uses a long baton and, partly through his studies with Nikisch and partly, one would think, through his own temperament, his gestures are economical and always to the point. One can hardly imagine a 'stiller' conductor. His movements are intended solely for the direction of the orchestra and never, in a showy way, for the edification of the audience.

One tends to think of Sir Adrian today mainly as a devoted interpreter of standard works – though perhaps he would dislike the description 'interpreter' and prefer some such term as 'presenter'. But it must be remembered that in his long career, particularly in his BBC days, he has performed every sort of music that has come along, from the classics to the most 'advanced' contemporary outpourings. The first concert performance in this country of Alban Berg's *Wozzeck*, for instance, was given by him a few years before the war, with May Blyth as the first British *Marie*.

In rehearsing contemporary works, he has always preferred, if possible, to have the composer present, so that his reading of the score might be as near as possible to its originator's wishes. On one occasion he spotted a decidedly odd passage in the score and, turning to the orchestra, asked, 'Is the composer here?' On being told that the composer was not present, Sir Adrian gave a sigh of resignation and said, 'Ah, well, I shall just have to play it as he wrote it' – faintly indicating, perhaps, that he did not think much of the piece but would do all he could.

It is on record, by the way, that 'Mr Adrian C Boult' gave concerts in Liverpool – with programmes embracing a Brandenburg Concerto and 'It's a Long Way to Tipperary' – at which the charge for admission was twopence. Those were very early days, just after the start of World War I – but one may be sure that the audience got a very good twopenn'orth.

After taking his degree at Oxford, the young Adrian Boult studied in Leipzig where the German conductor, Arthur Nikisch, made a profound impression upon him. He first attracted attention in London with his conducting of some Royal Philharmonic Society concerts before joining the staff of the Royal College of Music. He has toured a great deal abroad, making a special point of introducing British music to foreign audiences.

In the war days he carried his full share of the task of conducting the Proms, often under difficult conditions, and he won the warm affection and regard of audiences eager for the healing influence of the great classics at that grim time. One Last Night in particular he has reason to remember as an occasion on which the enthusiasm of the Prommers resulted in a decidedly awkward situation.

'When we had all left the platform,' he told me, 'it was raided by hyper-enthusiasts and bits of music as well as my two sticks were stolen as souvenirs. But my wife went at once to the artists' entrance, harangued the crowd outside and told them that sticks were irreplaceable in wartime, whereat they were promptly returned!'

After leaving the BBC in 1950 on reaching the age limit, Sir Adrian became principal conductor of the London Philharmonic Orchestra and still retains a close link with them.

In his personality and platform manner there is nothing of false modesty, no question of 'backing away into the limelight'. It is simply that the music is all that matters and that he sees no point in obtruding himself.

A typical instance of his attitude occurred at a party following a concert which had been shared with him by a visiting conductor. A photographer asked Sir Adrian to pose for a picture. 'Oh', he said, with his customary courtesy, 'you don't want a picture of me, do you? It's Mr Blank's evening. I'm always around.'

It is a good thing for the musical life of this country that Sir Adrian, still on top form, has been around for quite a time.

10

THE SHADOWS AGAIN

FOR THE 1943 season, the BBC Symphony Orchestra and the London Philharmonic were scheduled to appear under three conductors, Sir Henry Wood, Basil Cameron, and Sir Adrian Boult, but after two concerts Sir Henry, now seventy-four, was taken ill, and Cameron and Boult carried the season through, apart from a few concerts conducted by Wood towards the end.

This season there was for the first time a promenade concert on a Sunday. The Government announced that they needed the Royal Albert Hall on a Wednesday evening for a meeting in honour of China on the sixth anniversary of the Sino-Japanese War, and the Prom scheduled for that evening was accordingly transferred to the following Sunday. Nowadays the occasional Sunday Prom is deliberately planned to fit in with the engagements of visiting orchestras from abroad.

It was hoped to make the 1944 season a fitting celebration of the Golden Jubilee of the Proms – but Fate had further blows in store. Hitler had not yet finished his final fling against London and was sending over his flying-bombs, the 'doodle-bugs', with their evil roar, the cutting-out of their engines, the awful silence, and the sickening crash.

One morning, Basil Cameron, rehearsing the London Philharmonic in the Albert Hall, held up the score of the next work to be played – a march from Sir Arthur Bliss's film music.

'*Things to Come*', announced Mr Cameron – and immediately there was heard the macabre throb of a 'doodle-bug', followed by the silence and a shattering explosion close at hand. The bomb had fallen just behind Church Street, Kensington and, as it happens, Mr Cameron now lives in a flat only a stone's throw from that spot.

The concerts were carried on for a few more evenings in the Albert Hall until the authorities decided that the situation had become too hazardous and later concerts were broadcast by the BBC from Bedford.

From Bedford there came a concert with a particular poignancy – a performance of Beethoven's great Seventh Symphony (called by Wagner for some curious reason 'the apotheosis of the dance'), conducted by Sir Henry Wood. It was a masterly presentation of a masterpiece. Sir Adrian Boult said at the time that anyone listening at home might well have thought that it was conducted by a brilliant young man of forty.

It was Sir Henry's swan song. He had not been well for some time and he collapsed after the performance but did live long enough to be assured that the anniversary concert on 10th August had been safely broadcast.

Earlier that year, when Sir Henry had been guest of honour at a Savage Club lunch, a Brother Savage had written the lines :

A hundred seasons may elapse
Ere timber reach its prime.
Small wonder, then, we hope our Wood
Will go on beating time!

But Time, as is its way, eventually beat Sir Henry. He died just over a week after the anniversary concert, in the darkness of war but in the shining light of achievement.

If Sir Henry Wood had not lived, someone would have had to invent him – if, that is, the musical life of this country were to be as fruitful and rewarding as it proved to be through his efforts.

In his later years he was able to look back upon a life of service to music and to his fellow musicians. He had earned the gratitude of a host of composers and young performers whom he had encouraged at the outset of their careers. He had played a dominant part in the enormous advance in the standard of orchestral playing in this country. His devotion to the Royal Academy of Music had placed it for ever in his debt. He had lived to see the day when his concerts were heard by huge audiences on the radio.

For his Jubilee as a conductor in 1938, Vaughan Williams had composed the lovely *Serenade to Music*, in which the soloists were sixteen of the finest British singers of the day – Isobel Baillie, Stiles-Allen, Elsie Suddaby, Eva Turner; Margaret Balfour, Muriel Brunskill, Astra Desmond, Mary Jarred; Parry Jones, Heddle Nash, Frank Titterton, Walter Widdop; Norman Allin, Robert Easton, Roy Henderson, Harold Williams.

He was a knight and a Companion of Honour. But his greatest memorial is to be found in the eager faces of the young Prommers who, even today, owe so much to his efforts and inspiration.

As he would have wished, the 1945 season of Proms went on at the Royal Albert Hall, even though he was not there. But they were still, and always will be, the Henry Wood Promenade Concerts.

In the 1945 and 1946 seasons, a brilliant and colourful figure, Constant Lambert, came on the Prom scene as assistant conductor, with Cameron and Boult, and the BBC Symphony and London Symphony Orchestras.

Constant Lambert, whose death at the age of forty-five was a grievous loss to music and to the joy of life, was, while still at the Royal College of Music, the first British composer to be commissioned by Diaghilev to write a ballet, *Romeo and Juliet*. His best-known work is *The Rio Grande*, employing jazz idioms and written for chorus, orchestra, and piano solo. Indeed, it was so much associated with his name that he used to say that it was a millstone round his neck ('They don't seem to know that I have written anything else'). His own favourite work, and probably his finest, was *Summer's Last Will and Testament*, for baritone, chorus, and orchestra. Much of his work was in the world of ballet and he was one of the significant figures in the early days of what is now the Royal Ballet. Shortly before the war he wrote one of the most readable and entertaining books about music, *Music Ho!*

His enthusiasms embraced cats, railway engines, the Marx Brothers, and Beachcomber. He had an enormous sense of fun, particularly of the 'nonsense' sort, and I well recall an annual 'ceremony' in the 'Gluepot' on St David's Day when he would insist on pinning a huge leek on the hat of our common Welsh friend – common in the strict sense of the word! – C B Rees. C B used to sport two splendid black hats in those days, dubbed by Lambert his 'baroque' hat and his 'rococo' hat.

In each of those two seasons all the Sibelius symphonies were performed and, in 1946, all the symphonies that Vaughan Williams had then written. And a notable Prom début was that of Yehudi Menuhin, appropriately playing the Elgar Violin Concerto which, as the wonder boy of thirteen, he had played on that same platform with the composer conducting.

The Prom pattern around this time tended to be: Brahms or Tchaikovsky on Monday, instead of the long-established Wagner; Wagner on Tuesday and Thursday, linked with Berlioz, Liszt, Sibelius, and Richard Strauss; Bach, Handel, and Mozart on Wednesday; Beethoven on Friday; and Saturday a miscellaneous night.

Julian Herbage, introducing the 1947 season, had a glimpse of things to come, finding it 'tempting' to describe the season as a Festival.

'Could even Salzburg, in the palmy pre-war days', he wrote, 'offer us three orchestras, three principal conductors, to say nothing of an associate conductor, and composers directing their own works? It can safely be asserted that no such musical enterprise has previously been conceived.'

In contrast to Henry Wood's three rehearsals for an

entire week's concerts in the old days, each concert was to have an average of three.

The orchestras were the BBC Symphony, the London Philharmonic, and the London Symphony and the three principal conductors Sir Adrian Boult, Basil Cameron, and Sir Malcolm Sargent, with Stanford Robinson, who had long been associated with the BBC and had made a particular study of opera, as associate conductor. That season, for the first time, a Prom was televised.

In the years immediately following, Trevor Harvey, John Hollingsworth and Maurice Miles who had studied under Sir Henry Wood, and who himself became professor of conducting at the Royal Academy of Music, also took part in the Proms as assistant conductors.

But one cannot help wondering how many people realised, when Sir Malcolm Sargent first became a principal conductor of the Proms in 1947, just how powerful an impact he was to make upon Prommers in the years to come.

11

'WE WANT MALCOLM'

IT WAS AWAY back in 1921 that a brisk and purposeful young man, with dark hair, piercing eyes and an ugly-handsome face, walked on to the platform at Queen's Hall for his first appearance before a Prom audience. He was not particularly tall but his slender frame and lithe carriage gave the impression of height. Personality oozed from him and his whole manner spoke of pent-up energy and vitality.

A brisk bow to audience and orchestra and, with arms flying, he embarked on a composition of his own. It was called *An Impression of a Windy Day* and, when it had whirled to its conclusion, the audience insisted on hearing it again.

The young composer-conductor was given a big ovation, even though, at that early stage, the audience did not go so far as to shout 'We Want Malcolm'. But that was to happen year after year when he had taken his place as the darling of the Prommers and when the white carnation – the second white carnation at the Proms – had become his symbol.

Malcolm Sargent, who was to surprise a lot of people in the course of his career, had already surprised the members of the Queen's Hall Orchestra. He had first performed his orchestral piece with the

Leicester Symphony Orchestra, which he had formed
the previous year, and the piece had been heard by
Sir Henry Wood who had offered to include it in a
promenade concert programme.

Naturally delighted, the young composer had said
how honoured he was that his little work should be
conducted by Sir Henry. 'Oh,' Wood had replied,
'I'm not going to conduct it. You are.' When it came
to rehearsal, all that the orchestra knew about the
man whose work they were to perform was that he
was a Mus. Doc. They accordingly built up a mental
picture of someone rather elderly and pompous in an
academic sort of way – and were considerably shaken
when an ebullient fellow of twenty-six appeared on
the scene. He had in fact become a Doctor of Music,
the youngest in the country, two years earlier.

A gifted organist and pianist who had done some
conducting locally, he was now on the threshold of
the career which was to take him round the world
and to win him a secure place in the hearts of his
devoted Prom audiences.

It is not really surprising that Malcolm Sargent
should have been held in such sincere affection and
regard by the Prommers. For youth has always been
a characteristic of the Proms – youth of spirit if not
always of years – and Sargent, to the end of his days,
remained a young man, enthusiastic, interesting and
interested, boundlessly energetic, fond of company
and particularly the company of young people,
entertaining and ready to be entertained. He derived
a great deal of sheer joy from music and loved to
impart it to others. In this sense of presenting music
attractively, he was, as he freely admitted, a showman.

But, though Sargent was ever young in heart and in spirit, there was in later years much music being written by the younger generation of composers with which he was not 'in tune'. He said so quite frankly and explained that there was a wealth of music of the sort he loved, enough to keep him very busy, and that he was content to leave the other to younger conductors who would probably do it better.

This is not to say that he lacked adventure in the music he conducted. When, for instance, the Leeds Triennial Festival was presenting in 1931 the première of Walton's *Belshazzar's Feast*, which, in its brilliance and barbaric colour, was sensationally far removed from the established idea of an oratorio, the choir threatened to go on strike at being faced with such wildly unconventional stuff. Called to the rescue, Sargent immediately assimilated the score, pulled things together and gave a shattering performance of the work, a work which he continued to conduct from time to time throughout his career. Walton (later Sir William) was his friend for life and, when his opera, *Troilus and Cressida*, was to have its première at Covent Garden in 1954, it was to Sargent, who had not conducted in an opera house for many years, that he entrusted it.

Sargent's instinct for getting along with young people without ever talking down to them – perhaps it was partly because he did not talk down to them – was never more in evidence or put to better purpose than in the children's concerts which he gave in association with Robert Mayer. Years before Leonard Bernstein was so successful in this sphere in America, Malcolm Sargent was chatting like an amiable big brother to great audiences in the Central Hall, Westminster, asking members of the orchestra to stand up and demonstrate what each individual instrument sounded like, pointing out in the most fluent and readily understandable way the details which should be observed, and always radiating the joy and satisfaction to be derived from great music. It was all done in a charming and unschoolmasterly way which unfailingly held the interest of the children, many of whom must surely be among the Prom audiences of today.

There was always something of the schoolboy about Malcolm Sargent himself and it was certainly not his least endearing characteristic. He could even boast like a schoolboy, as when he would come bouncing back from a holiday and declare: 'I've been playing a lot of tennis and, d'you know, I've beaten fellows years younger than myself', adding, in a ruefully qualifying way, 'I usually lose by serving double faults'. Or it might be: 'Oh, I've sailed every kind of boat – catamarans, everything – great fun, you know'. This was the schoolboy, bubbling over at his achievement and determined to let you know about it. He enjoyed a saucy joke, very often a joke which, far from being subtle and sophisticated, was decidedly of the schoolboy order.

He revelled in being physically fit for his job. 'You know', he would say, 'I'm not like the businessman who has been sitting at a desk all the week and has to take exercise by playing golf at the week-end. I get my exercise by waving my arms about for hours on end when I'm working. When I relax, I put my feet up and read a book'.

Much of his satisfaction at his physical stamina may well have derived from the fact that, when in his thirties, he was desperately ill – at a time when tuberculosis was a killer – and that he not only overcame the onset but functioned for the rest of his career on one lung.

Sir Malcolm liked to be liked. He enjoyed being famous and he loved applause – as do most people, though few are so frank about it. He appreciated elegant living and good food, while not being a big eater. A glass or two of wine with a meal was all he drank and he smoked only the occasional cigar after a meal.

The same man could get to the heart of the music he loved – he was an unusually quick learner of a score – and convey it to his audience. There was nothing inconsistent in all this. It was the same man, for he was an unsubtle character.

One of his great strengths was in his handling of large choral forces – he was adored in Huddersfield and by the Royal Choral Society, of which he was conductor for nearly thirty years. He could bring together these hundreds of singers and persuade them to sing far better than they ever thought they could; and it was all done by a combination of technique and belief.

There is no doubt that Malcolm Sargent had a simple religious faith which buoyed him up through life. Among a group of his friends having lunch in the Beefsteak Club – a typical gathering might consist of a judge, an MP, an ex-Governor-General, a business tycoon and a writer – he could discuss and argue about metaphysics. But his own faith was a simple and sincere one.

When rehearsing some great oratorio, he really did believe the words that were being sung and could explain their meaning and tell his choir how, technically, they could convey that meaning.

This was not always easy, as was apparent in a story he enjoyed telling. Rehearsing Elgar's *The Dream of Gerontius*, a work very close to his heart, he was explaining to a rather stolid tenor that in the first part of the work Gerontius is on earth, but that in the second part he actually comes face to face with an angel and that therefore a different quality of voice, a more awed tone, must be employed. 'Ah yes, Sir Malcolm – thank you', said the tenor – and briskly wrote in the appropriate place in his score: 'Meet angel'.

With his unfailing sense of timing, Harold Malcolm Watts Sargent chose a significant year in which to be born – 1895, a few months before the first season of promenade concerts was launched in Queen's Hall. He came into the world just when Sir Henry Wood and Robert Newman were planning their first programmes and he made his last appearance before the public on the platform of the Proms at the Royal Albert Hall.

Though it was in the charming historic town of Stamford, in Lincolnshire, that he spent his childhood and youth and though he always regarded it as his birthplace, he was not in fact born there. His mother was on a brief visit from Stamford to Ashford, in Kent, when the young Malcolm appeared on the scene; but Stamford was his much-loved home town.

It would seem that, from his boyhood days, there was never really any question of his spending his life other than in the world of music, though he did have a choice of careers within that sphere. His father, Harry Sargent, was a clerk with a firm of builder's merchants but, more important from the point of view of his son's future, he was also organist and choirmaster at St John's Church, Stamford, where young Malcolm regularly lent a hand pumping the organ.

While still at Stamford School, Malcolm took his ARCO diploma. From a lady with the charmingly appropriate name of Miss Tinkler he received his first piano lessons and, as she was the rehearsal accompanist for the local amateur operatic society, he used to turn over the pages for her and eventually helped with the accompanying.

It was with this amateur society that he made his first appearance as a conductor when, the regular conductor having failed to turn up for a performance of *The Gondoliers*, it was suggested, more in jest than earnest, that young Sargent might take over. He did, and things went so well that he became the regular conductor of the society.

Through the years, Malcolm Sargent never lost his love for the Gilbert and Sullivan operettas. He was later associated with the D'Oyly Carte Company, busying himself in improving the musical standard of the performances, and throughout his life he would return from time to time to conduct the occasional performance. No one was a greater authority on the operettas than he. 'D'you know', he once said enthusiastically to me, 'when I conduct Gilbert and Sullivan I feel forty years younger.'

He was articled to Dr Keeton, of Peterborough

Cathedral as an organ student and he took up his first official appointment when he was nineteen as organist at Melton Mowbray Parish Church at a salary of £80 a year, an appointment he continued to hold for ten years, although engaged also in other activities, including service in the Durham Light Infantry in World War I ('No rank – just one of the file').

Reports of his prowess as a pianist reached the ears of Benno Moisiewitsch who invited him to come and play to him and, assuring him that he could enjoy a distinguished career as a concert pianist, proceeded to give him lessons without charging any fees. But it was then that there occurred the significant episode of his conducting *An Impression of a Windy Day* at the Proms and Sir Henry Wood's insistence that he was a born conductor.

'So, you see', he once told me, 'it was Benno who snatched me from the organ-loft and Henry Wood who snatched me from the keyboard. But I do believe that I could have been quite happy as a church organist'.

He was only twenty-seven when he was appointed conductor of the orchestral class at the Royal College of Music and, as he still had commitments in Lincolnshire entailing travel between the two centres, he economised by arranging his overnight stays in London with half-price bed and breakfast accommodation at a small hotel near the College where, the guests having departed to their bedrooms, his bed would be made up on top of the bath in one of the public bathrooms.

In the years that followed, he embraced an enormous

number of activities, being appointed a conductor of the British National Opera Company, giving the first public performance of Vaughan Williams's opera *Hugh the Drover* at His Majesty's Theatre, beginning his long and close association with the Royal Choral Society at the Royal Albert Hall, and taking on the musical directorship of the Courtauld–Sargent Concerts, which won a great reputation at Queen's Hall, bringing to London such artists as Schnabel, Horowitz, Milstein, Klemperer, Szell, and a host of others. While responsible for the overall musical direction, Sargent conducted some of the concerts and the visiting conductors the others.

In 1932, Sir Thomas Beecham embarked on the formation of the London Philharmonic Orchestra and called in Malcolm Sargent as his assistant, thus starting a long-standing acquaintance between the two. As was his wont, Beecham revelled throughout his life in telling stories 'against' Sargent – stories which Sargent, as a wise man, cheerfully retold.

It is believed, for instance, that it was Beecham who originated the nickname 'Flash Harry', curtailed in later years to the more affectionate 'Flash' – indeed, placards bearing the words 'We Want Flash' were often held up in the arena during the jollifications on Last Nights of the Proms.

The story goes that both Beecham and Sargent were giving concerts with the same orchestra in a town in the provinces, Sargent rehearsing in the morning and Beecham in the afternoon. Finding the orchestra in somewhat lethargic form, Beecham admonished them: 'What has Flash Harry been doing to you this morning?'

Sir Malcolm used to tell how, when he had been describing in an after-dinner speech an occasion on which his car had been fired on by Arabs during the troubles in Palestine, Sir Thomas took out his cigar and murmured: 'I had not realised that the Arabs were so musical'.

And there was Beecham's remark on being told that Sargent had been conducting highly successful concerts in Tokyo: 'Flash in Japan, eh!'

When, after Beecham's death, Sir Malcolm was to conduct a service in his memory, one London newspaper, recalling a couple of Beecham's 'anti-Sargent' stories, commented that it would seem that Sir Malcolm had buried the hatchet, to which Sargent promptly replied that there was no question of there being a hatchet to bury and that, if it came to Beecham stories, he knew many much better ones that Sir Thomas had told 'against' him. They were in fact friends for years and, sharing the same birthday, though not of the same year, they always exchanged greetings telegrams, wherever in the world they happened to be.

Sir Malcolm's extensive tours in many parts of the world before, during and after the war – in a single year he might cover some forty thousand miles – earned for him the title of 'Britain's Ambassador of Music'. For one wartime visit to Sweden he travelled in the questionable luxury of the bomb-rack of a Mosquito aircraft. On a postwar visit to Moscow and Leningrad he met Shostakovich who granted him permission to give the first three performances outside Russia of his then unfinished *Symphony No 11*. He toured with British orchestras or appeared as guest conductor with famous foreign orchestras in their own countries. He had friends in most parts of the world, but he remained essentially an Englishman.

I remember discussing with him the fact that the Royal Choral Society's concerts always begin with the singing of several verses of the National Anthem, but, while agreeing that this was sometimes criticised, he was quite unrepentant.

'I know it is sometimes said to be old-fashioned and out of date', he said, 'but I am all in favour of it. After all, don't people want the "knavish tricks" to be frustrated and the Queen's enemies scattered and made to fall!'

He was in Australia when war broke out in 1939 and, against the persuasion of his friends there and in some doubt about the place music would have in wartime, he came straight home. And, far from finding any sagging of interest, he was as busy as ever during the war years. All over the country he played his part in bringing much-needed music to the people. Typical of him was his comment when the air-raid warning had sounded: 'Anybody who wants to go can do so now. But the orchestra will carry on. We may be killed, but we shall be playing something that Hitler can never kill'.

Fine musician though he was, Sir Malcolm was never one to bury himself away out of touch with life itself. That was why, as a member of the BBC's Brains Trust, he always had something interesting to say on whatever might be under discussion. Through that medium he became known, almost as a personal friend, to millions of people who had no particular interest in music. When the talk did turn to music he spoke, of course, with vast authority but always in a way readily understood by the layman.

A man of strong personality and mercurial wit, Sargent left his mark on a conversation as surely as in a concert hall. In the intimacy of his own flat, just over the road from the Royal Albert Hall, he was the perfect host, with the gift of 'circulating' in a party and contributing to half a dozen different conversations, so that every departing guest was saying to himself: 'He spent the entire evening talking to me'.

It was on one of those occasions that Sir Malcolm told me a story of his very early days as a conductor.

'After one of my concerts, a critic wrote that I had given a "perfunctory" performance of a certain work', he said. 'I was annoyed about it and pointed out that, whereas he was entitled to give an opinion about my performance, to say that it was "perfunctory" was to suggest that I had not given proper attention to the job I was paid to do.

'Some time later, the same critic wrote a notice of another of my concerts. He began, "If one did not know that Malcolm Sargent takes meticulous care over the preparation of his concerts, one might have thought that this was a perfunctory performance——'

'There was nothing else for it. We became friends and remained so through the years.'

In that flat one could meet Sir Malcolm's pet budgerigar, Hughie. As budgies do not live for ever, he had a succession of them and they were all called Hughie, after the small boy who gave him the first one. He was a great animal-lover, a member of the

(*Above*) An impression of the first concert at the Queen's Hall, London, in December 1893. (*Below*) The Queen's Hall after World War II bombs had reduced it to a shell.

(*Above*) Sir Adrian Boult conducting the BBC Symphony Orchestra at the last night of the fifty-third Henry Wood Promenade Season in 1947. (*Below*) Sir Adrian, three years later, with his leader Paul Beard, shortly before Sir Adrian's retirement as conductor-in-chief of the BBC Symphony Orchestra.

council of the Zoo and president of the Royal Society for the Prevention of Cruelty to Animals.

In that flat, too, one could inspect his fine library of orchestral scores, a considerable development from the first one he ever possessed, a tattered piano score of *Messiah*, which cost him one penny out of his pocket money.

Surrounded by his treasures, he would chat about this and that. About, for instance, the music of today: 'Now, let's get this straight', he would say. 'In the whole history of music there has always been more bad music than good. Today, as more people are writing music than ever before, there is more bad music being written. There is a lot I do not consider to be very good. I am not against it's being performed but I am rather busy doing the other stuff. I do feel that the younger people ought to be better at playing the younger music. And just because I do not do a piece it does not mean that it is bad. I am lucky, you know, in that I happen to have lived in a magnificent era. There were Elgar, Vaughan Williams, Delius, and Holst. What a quartet! No other country could match them within the thirty years' limit. And since then, of course, we have the splendid music of Britten and Walton.'

Or perhaps he would reveal an unrealised ambition: 'Before I die I would like to put Elgar's oratorios, *The Apostles* and *The Kingdom*, on the map as accepted works. I know them to be masterpieces but they are not yet accepted as such.'

Sir Malcolm performed many quiet acts of generosity, though it was never from him that one heard about them, and, apart from the practical help

I

he gave to many private individuals, he was one of the few conductors to vary his fee according to circumstances. If he particularly wanted to do a concert or was sympathetic to a cause, the financial side would not deter him. There are choral societies in the Midlands and North which, to a considerable extent, owe their continued existence to him. He enjoyed so much working with them that he would often charge a very low fee.

But this was the private side of Sir Malcolm Sargent. In the minds of the vast majority of people the image of him that will linger in their affections for years to come is that of the slim, elegant figure walking smartly up the slope from the conductor's room to the podium of the Royal Albert Hall, white carnation in lapel and fingers toying with his cuff as though he were about to produce a rabbit from nowhere. It was while he was chief conductor of the BBC Symphony Orchestra, from 1950 until 1957, that he made his indelible mark on the Proms and, even after he had given up the official appointment, he remained the central figure to the end.

The white carnation had its own story to tell. Some fifteen years ago a young man of seventeen, lying paralysed in a London hospital and knowing that he was dying, wrote to Sir Malcolm, telling him how much he enjoyed listening to his broadcast concerts. Sir Malcolm wrote back – busy as he was, he always seemed to find time to answer letters – and a correspondence developed. When the young man died in 1950 he left a sum of money with the request that it should be used to buy Sir Malcom's carnation for every concert he conducted. Said Sir Malcolm:

130

'He was a very courageous boy. We never met, just wrote to each other. Since his death I have worn the carnation for him'.

And, of course, Prommers will always remember Sir Malcom's friendly but firm control of the more exuberant elements in the crowd on the many Last Nights over which he presided. He liked to see them enjoying themselves but he knew exactly how to check any high-spirited outbursts which might occur at the wrong moment. Experienced Prommers have always, of course, known how to behave, but sometimes a new boy would blow a whistle or burst a balloon at an inappropriate time when Sir Malcolm was speaking. 'I don't think we want that, thank you', he would say, or 'Will the nanny please take those toys away?', to be greeted by a rousing cheer – and then silence.

There is an admirable recording, taken from BBC archives (BBC Radio Enterprises) of the closing stages of the last Prom which Sir Malcolm conducted in September 1966. It most aptly captures the exhilarating mood of the occasion, including the *Sea-Songs*, *Rule Britannia*, *Jerusalem*, and Sir Malcolm's little speech at the end, followed, of course, by the shouts of 'We want Malcolm' and the singing of *For He's a Jolly Good Fellow*. The version of *Rule Britannia* used at the Proms, by the way, was arranged by Sargent from Thomas Arne's original melody and was first heard when he conducted it in the opening concert of the Royal Festival Hall.

Not long before the onset of his fatal illness, Sir Malcolm had carried out an arduous visit to Australia, where he conducted all of Beethoven's symphonies and concertos and threw in Walton's *Belshazzar's Feast* for good measure.

Deeply distressed though he was at missing the opening night of the 1967 season – it would have been his twenty-first opening Prom – he clung to the hope that he might be able to conduct at least some of the concerts. But it was not long before he realised the worst and he never showed stauncher courage than in those last days. When, supported by his doctors, he made that sad last appearance, seen by six thousand people in the Royal Albert Hall and by millions of television viewers, he knew that the end of the road was near.

One of the last letters which Malcolm Sargent wrote was posted on the night before he died. 'As you know', he wrote to a friend, 'my news is very bad, and I made the Last Night through the sheer tenacity of my doctors, who gave me seven and a half hours of injections – a sort of Esso, and the tiger in my tank did wonders.' His courage, and even his wit, never deserted him.

Though there was an impressive memorial service in Westminster Abbey, those of us who attended the service in All Saints' Church, Stamford – just at the end of the narrow All Saints' Street where Malcolm Sargent lived as a boy – felt a certain rightness about its simplicity. The music had been chosen by Sir Malcolm and the mood was not so much of sadness as of hope.

The grass verge around the thirteenth-century church was banked with flowers, many of them from people who had never met Sir Malcolm – 'a police-woman in Cornwall', for instance, and a lover of Sir

Malcolm's broadcasts 'in gratitude from one house-bound, for whom the door never closed'.

And from London there came Vivien Banfield, the eighteen-year-old piano student who had been seen by millions of viewers when she presented a bouquet to Sir Malcolm on his last appearance at the Royal Albert Hall. She brought carnations, fashioned in the form of a treble clef and bearing the inscription 'To Sir Malcolm, from "his children" at the Promenade Concerts'.

That, perhaps, was the tribute that would have pleased him most.

12

MARCHING ON

I T IS SOMETIMES said, with a nostalgic sigh: 'But the Proms are not what they *were*'.

Of course they are not. They could not be, and still go on. They are not the Proms of 1895, so exactly poised for the start of London's greatest adventure in music. They are not the Proms as later developed by Henry Wood and Robert Newman, with an unfailing combination of artistry, imagination, and finger-on-the-public-pulse. They are not the Proms of 1927, when the BBC took over the administrative responsibility but with Sir Henry Wood still the dominant figure. They are not the Proms of 1941 when, perforce, they were translated from the intimacy of Queen's Hall into the wider spaces of the Royal Albert Hall. They are certainly not the Proms of even as recently as 1959.

Beethoven and Wagner no longer hold sway on Friday and Monday nights respectively. But neither is dethroned. Wagner comes in from time to time for very full representation and Beethoven, his value as a reliable anchor-man for almost any concert fully appreciated, spreads his empire across the programmes in general.

And the Proms go on – with enormous success.

They go on because, changed though they are, they have retained their qualities of youthfulness and of being not only in tune with time and fashion but also of having an ear for the future. There are interesting parallels between the approach of today and the experience of Henry Wood. 'Progress' does not mean merely the presentation of 'novelties', using the word in the sense of first performances, but also the presentation of great things of the past alongside interesting things of the present.

One might well ask of many of the novelties which have been presented at the Proms throughout the years 'Where are you now?' – as one might ask of Amy Woodford Finden's *Indian Love Lyrics* themselves. But the important thing is that great numbers of works have contributed to the flow of the Proms. Some have sunk without trace, some have survived, and some are worth reviving. All have played their part in the adventurous life-force of the Proms.

It took Henry Wood many years of perseverance before, while encouraging contemporary composers and presenting what was then new, he could be sure of attracting a good house when playing the music of Bach. At the Proms today, while being given the opportunity of facing the challenges of Messaien, Boulez, and Stockhausen, we are being made very conscious of composers like, for instance, Monteverdi and Haydn, neither of them exactly a new boy. The Proms have changed enormously but they still possess much of the same essential spirit.

One of the major influences in the 1950–60 period was the increase in the number of orchestras taking part, an obvious advantage in that each could bring to the Proms works which they had already meticulously rehearsed and performed. The Royal

Philharmonic were there in 1952 and, in the Diamond Jubilee Season of the Proms two years later, their exuberant founder, Sir Thomas Beecham, made his début, conducting two concerts.

In 1953, Sir John Barbirolli brought his famed Hallé Orchestra to the Proms for the first time and it is hardly surprising that he and the 'Hallé Band' rapidly became one of the most popular ingredients of later seasons. There is everything in the personality and great ability of Barbirolli – 'Glorious John' as Vaughan Williams called him – to appeal to Prom audiences. And, anyhow, it was not his own personal début – was he not a 'cellist under 'Old Timber' at Queen's Hall in his early days?

Few experiences can be more exhilarating than to listen to Sir John – seventy in 1969, the centenary year of Henry Wood's birth – as he reminisces about his life in that gruff, kindly voice of his. His early background was both romantic and significant. His father was Italian, his mother French; and young John (or, Giovanni Battista, to give him his real name) was born in London's Southampton Row, over what was then a baker's shop and is now a public house.

When Toscanini was starting his career as principal 'cellist in the orchestra of a little town near Padua, grandfather Barbirolli was the leader and his son the principal of the second violins. Both were playing in the orchestra of La Scala, Milan, when Verdi's *Otello* was first presented there in 1887 and, though not on that occasion, they did play at other times under the baton of Verdi himself. How's that for musical ancestry?

137

'Later, in London, my father and grandfather shared the first desk in the orchestra of the old Empire Theatre, Leicester Square, in the great days of Adeline Genée, the dancer', Sir John told me. 'Dad used to take me to the rehearsals there when I was four or five. In those days the conductor used to wear white gloves and sit down while he was conducting, and when I got home I would pinch a pair of my mother's or sister's gloves, lock the door, and sing away and conduct like mad.

'I used to go and listen to the bands in Lincoln's Inn Fields, near where we lived, and when the performance was over I would stand where the conductor had stood and wish that some day I might achieve fame by conducting in that bandstand!'

He has gone rather further than that bandstand and indeed has conducted almost every great orchestra and is one of the most highly regarded conductors on the world scene.

But, even though it was his firm ambition to be a conductor, he had wide experience as a 'cellist in his early days. By the time he was twelve he had played all the Beethoven quartets. ('Not many conductors or composers – and damn few critics – could say that they had done that by the time they were twelve', was his chuckling comment). Playing on a three-quarter size 'cello, he was soloist in a concerto in Queen's Hall when he was twelve, and a year later he played the Saint-Saëns concerto in the same hall.

When he was only fourteen he was playing in the theatre pit, and two years later he became the youngest member of the Queen's Hall Orchestra under Henry Wood. His link with the Proms could hardly have

138

started much earlier. But he went on to do a great deal of chamber music and solo playing and, under Dan Godfrey in Bournemouth, he gave the second performance of the 'cello concerto by Elgar, whom he adored and under whose baton he played in performances of *The Dream of Gerontius* and many works in the symphonic repertoire.

It is, however, as a great conductor and orchestra-builder that we think of Sir John today and his start in this field came when he founded the Barbirolli String Orchestra, going on to conduct many of the leading orchestras in the concert hall and the opera house. The first opera he conducted at Covent Garden, by the way, was *Madam Butterfly*, of which he quite recently made one of the finest of all recordings.

One of the most significant moves in his career happened in 1936. When Arturo Toscanini retired from the posts of musical director and permanent conductor of the New York Philharmonic, it was the London-born Italian John Barbirolli who was chosen to succeed him.

'I am very English and very Italian', he says. Indeed, when New York had first made his acquaintance, a newspaper described him as being 'as British as mutton chops or cricket'; on the other hand, it is not without pride that he recalls that a critic wrote of one of his performances in South America that it was 'more Barbirolli than John'. He won great acclaim in America – where he is a very welcome visitor today – and did much to familiarise American audiences with British music, his programmes including, for instance, first performances of Benjamin Britten's Violin Concerto and *Sinfonia da Requiem*.

But the war days made him more conscious than ever of his Britishness.

He came back for a few months to give a series of benefit concerts for British orchestral musicians and when, in 1943, he was invited to return to take on the task of rebuilding the famed Hallé Orchestra, he readily agreed. So began the work which he has carried out to such magnificent effect. (He was, by the way, able to celebrate the centenary of the foundation of his great orchestra by reproducing at a Prom the original programme of 'Mr Hallé's Grand Orchestral Concert' of 1858.)

If you ask Sir John about his own favourites among the composers, he understandably stresses the catholicity of his tastes. 'After all, I started early', he says. 'Only the other day I came across a score of the prelude to *Tristan and Isolde* which I had annotated when I was twelve. I was conducting Alban Berg as early as 1924 – before the mothers and fathers of some of the critics of today had even met!'

He *is* prepared to give you a hint, however, of some of the music for which he has a particular affection by quoting a 'special choice' programme he once gave – 'the sort of concert I might like to conduct if I thought it was my last'. The works were: Vaughan Williams's *Fantasia on a Theme of Thomas Tallis*, Delius's *Fennimore and Gerda*, Debussy's *La Mer*, and Elgar's Second Symphony.

The list provides some hints but it tells only part of the story. The Finnish Government, for instance, awarded him one of their highest honours, making him Commander (First Class) of the Order of the White Rose for what he has done for the music of

140

Sibelius, not only in Britain, but throughout the world; and when he is on his many visits to Berlin the music they particularly ask him to play is that of Haydn, Beethoven, Brahms, and Mahler. Nor must we forget, of course, his love for the great operas and his gift for conducting them. Indeed, one wishes that he had time for more activity in the opera house in these later years.

Elgar, Vaughan Williams and Sibelius come very high in his list of affections. 'As happened with Richard Strauss', he says, 'the deaths of these three great composers were followed by periods of denigration. But they are immortals – and it is a physical fact that you can't kill immortality.'

Anyone who has listened to a Barbirolli concert has experienced the enormous emotional impact that his music-making has upon the audience; but in order to produce that effect he sets about his task in an utterly professional and practical way. Though a firm discipli-narian, he has the highest regard and respect for his orchestral players and does not believe in talking a lot of airy-fairy stuff to them at rehearsal. He knows exactly what effect he wishes to achieve and to his players he talks only technical facts about how it can be brought about.

For Sir John is both great conductor and great orchestral *teacher*, as his achievement with the Hallé has shown. When other leading British orchestras are appearing at the Proms, it is worth realising that a remarkable number of the principal and sub-principal players are former members of the 'Hallé Band', chosen and trained by Barbirolli. That is a matter of great pride and satisfaction to Sir John.

141

No audience is more conscious than the Prommers that great orchestras consist of highly talented individuals, carefully chosen and working as a team. However brilliant the conductor, he would look somewhat ridiculous, standing there and waving his arms about, if the orchestra had nothing to offer. Wise conductors know it and regard their players not as servants but as colleagues. They know that first-class orchestral players, being professionals, will always play up to a certain standard, otherwise they would be letting *themselves* down. They know, too, that when the players demonstrate not only their technical skill but also their regard for the conductor and therefore their willing understanding of what he is aiming at, marvels can happen.

From Henry Wood's days the Prom audience has been encouraged to recognise individual players, to appreciate their work and to regard them as friends, and through the years there has been an impressive parade of splendid instrumentalists, many of whom have, of course, appeared as soloists as well as members of orchestras at the Proms – people like Charles Woodhouse, Arthur Catterall, Marie Wilson, Marie, Sidonie and Leon Goossens, Aubrey and Dennis Brain, Frederick Thurston, Alec Whittaker, Archie Camden, Anthony Pini, Jack Brymer, Hugh Bean, to mention only a few from the long list. And, of course, Paul ('We want Paul') Beard.

Many Prommers must retain a warm affection for Paul Beard, a brilliant violoinist who deliberately chose the path of the orchestral leader rather than that of the soloist and who led the BBC Symphony Orchestra for twenty-six years up to his retirement in

1962. He, on his part, has a permanent reminder of the affection of the Prommers. When he returns to his home at Ewell after a round of golf – his other passion – he picks up a silver-backed brush and comb presented to him by his well-wishers.

Paul Beard was a very early starter as a musician. He was taught violin and viola by his father, who was for many years principal viola in the City of Birmingham Orchestra. At the age of six, in velvet suit with lace collar, Paul made his first appearance in public, playing three violin solos. When he was eighteen, he was appointed principal viola of the Birmingham Orchestra, his father proudly and happily moving down to make way for him; at twenty, he was leading the orchestra.

It was Sir Thomas Beecham who called him from Birmingham to lead the London Philharmonic Orchestra, which he had just founded. Four years later he succeeded Arthur Catterall as leader of the BBC Symphony Orchestra, chosen by Sir Adrian Boult, that wise judge of orchestral players for their ability, their experience, and their sense of loyal duty.

In the 1950's, the Royal Liverpool Philharmonic, the Bournemouth Symphony and the BBC Opera Orchestra were among those which took part – and appropriate to the spirit of the Proms – the National Youth Orchestra of Great Britain also gave a concert.

In the 1953 season, during which the over-all representation of British works was more than a quarter of the whole output, the bold step was taken of omitting the *Sea Songs* from the main part of the programme of the last night. They were, however, played as an encore at the end. But they were back the following year, with the explanation that they had been left out because it had been felt that 'the accompaniment provided by certain elements of the audience was tending to make their performance more of a nuisance than a pleasure to both the main audience in the hall and to broadcast listeners'. But now they were back in the main body of the programme, 'there being little doubt now that the exuberance of the occasion will not exceed reasonable bounds'.

Opportunities were seized upon for the celebration of anniversaries and other significant events. A performance of *The Dream of Gerontius* marked the centenary of Elgar's birth, and, in the same year (1957), the great Norwegian soprano, Kirsten Flagstad, came out of retirement to make her only Prom appearance, singing some Grieg songs on the fiftieth anniversary of the composer's death.

In the Puccini centenary year (1958), the third act of *Tosca* was presented, the first time a complete act from one of his operas had been given at the Proms. Sir Malcolm Sargent conducted a concert in memory of Sibelius, who had died the previous year. There was also an anniversary of particular domestic interest – the centenary of the birth of Robert Newman, the founder of the Proms. The programme consisted of works known to have been favourites of his, and it is intriguing to note what they were: Wagner's *Die Meistersinger* Overture; 'Softly Awakes my Heart' from Saint-Saëns' *Samson and Delilah*; Rachmaninov's *Rhapsody on a Theme of Paganini* (the soloist, Benno Moiseiwitsch, also played some piano pieces); Dvorak's

Two off-duty photographs of one of the best-loved Promenade personalities: Sir Malcolm Sargent with his secretary, Miss Sylvia Darley, and his pet budgerigar, Hughie, and (*Left*) with a friendly dolphin in the Sea Life Park, Makapuu, Hawaii in 1964.

The majestic figure of Leopold Stokowski conducting the BBC Symphony Orchestra at the Albert Hall in 1963. He was the first non-British conductor to appear for a complete Promenade Concert.

Symphony No 2; Delius's *Dance Rhapsody*; the whole topped off with Tchaikovsky's *1812*.

John Ireland's eightieth birthday was celebrated in 1959, and in the same season all nine symphonies of Vaughan Williams were performed. Four concerts were devoted to works by 'Masters of the Twentieth Century': Prokofiev, Bartok, Vaughan Williams, Richard Strauss, Ravel, Janacek, Stravinsky, Walton, Sibelius, Kodaly, Shostakovitch, Holst, Berg, Debussy, and Hindemith. Benjamin Britten, apparently, was not yet considered to have arrived in that category! Indeed, in the whole of that season he was represented only by the *Variations on a Theme of Purcell* (*The Young Person's Guide to the Orchestra*).

K

13

PROMS INTERNATIONAL

THE SIGNIFICANCE OF the appointment in 1959 of Mr William Glock as the BBC's Controller of Music is evidence of the immense change in the pattern of the Proms in the last few years. He is a fine pianist, a pupil of Schnabel; he made his own Prom début just before the war. He is a man of ideas with a will as strong as his determined jaw-line, and, from the start, he demonstrated that under his régime the Proms were certainly not going to be lacking in the spirit of adventure. It is said that, when he was music critic of a newspaper, Mr Glock was told that he was writing too much about Bartok and that he must not mention him again. He wrote about Bartok – and left.

The programmes for the 1959 season had already been planned when Mr Glock took office and it was therefore not until the following season that he really began to make his mark upon the Proms with a policy that seems to have had a general plan while being adaptable to the various developments as time went on.

That year of 1960, in which Mr Glock called for an enthusiastic campaign to make the season 'a landmark in the history of the Proms', provided many clues to the programme pattern as we know it today.

147

With some exceptions, single composers and single periods of music were no longer to have evenings to themselves. True, there was an evening of Haydn's *Creation* and a Gilbert and Sullivan evening on a Saturday, but otherwise the indication was that the whole field of music was to be explored, from the earliest days to the most 'advanced'. Works by different composers and from different periods were to be placed alongside each other, not of course haphazardly, but presenting them as all part of the musical 'family'.

There would still be first performances in the old sense of the 'novelty', but clearly greater stress was being laid on 'first Prom performances', the bringing into the Prom season of great numbers of works of today and of many yesterdays ago, which had never before been heard in these concerts.

For the first time, there was a concert performance of a complete opera, Stravinsky's *Oedipus Rex*, which had been a great success at Sadler's Wells; it brought to the Proms a young conductor named Colin Davis, now the principal conductor of the BBC Symphony Orchestra and consequently a significant figure in the Prom picture. In addition to this work, Stravinsky was represented by his *Symphony in C* and *Symphony in Three Movements*. Schoenberg's *Orchestral Variations* were there and Webern's *Six Orchestral Pieces*; and there were works by, for instance, Alban Berg, Roberto Gerhard, Charles Ives, Humphrey Searle, and Stockhausen. But there, too, were Beethoven's *Missa Solemnis* and Berlioz' *Grande Messe des Morts*. Beethoven, escaping from the confines of Friday nights, brought his weight to bear on fifteen programmes. There were nine guest conductors, many of them of the younger brigade, and the orchestra of the Royal Opera House, Covent Garden, made its first Prom appearance.

Not everyone who attended or listened to concerts in the 1961 season can have realised the full significance of the BBC's decision to discontinue the 'Nine O'clock News', a decision that caused quite an outcry from many radio listeners who resented the disappearance of an institution to which they had become so accustomed through the years. By the programme planners of the Proms it was hailed as a blessed release from a straitjacket. No longer had the items in the programmes to be so timed and arranged as to leave the 'sacred' hour of nine free for the broadcasting of the news. Beethoven's Ninth ('Choral') Symphony could be given after the interval instead of, absurdly, in the earlier part of the evening, with nothing but anticlimax to follow.

There were about sixty important works never before performed at the Proms, and, at the end of their season, Glyndebourne Festival Opera came into the picture for the first time with their completely polished performance of *Don Giovanni*.

The biggest attendance of the season was for a concert which included Schoenberg's Violin Concerto, a fact which drew from Mr Glock the comment: 'The lesson here was quite unmistakable: that Prommers welcome new experiences so long as they can also have the great music of the past that they know and love – in this case, Beethoven's Seventh Symphony'.

A cynic might have commented that the programme also included Debussy's *La Mer*, and that, in order to hear Beethoven's Seventh and *La Mer*, the audience

149

would cheerfully 'put up with' Schoenberg's Violin Concerto. Be that as it may, the satisfying truth is that there was a huge audience for Schoenberg, Beethoven, and Debussy – or, if you like, Beethoven, Debussy, and Schoenberg. It depends how you look at it; but facts are facts.

There were seventeen guest conductors in this season – a far cry from Sir Henry Wood and the Queen's Hall Orchestra – and four works specially commissioned from British composers; and the search for what was worthwhile in the earlier repertory brought forth an increasing representation of Haydn symphonies. The BBC Northern Orchestra joined the steadily growing Prom forces and, in the following year, the Philharmonia (now the New Philharmonia) and the BBC Scottish Orchestras were there.

Stravinsky's eightieth birthday was duly celebrated (1962), and Glyndebourne Opera presented their *Cosi Fan Tutte*, an indication that some full-length and fully-rehearsed operas were to be features of the Proms. This automatically brought in more foreign singers and conductors.

The international aspect of the Proms, to which we are now accustomed, was fully confirmed in the 1963 season with the appearances of foreign conductors for the first time. They made an impressive array – Georg Solti, the Hungarian musical director of Covent Garden Opera, bringing that company to the Proms for the first time with the whole of the third act of *Götter-dämmerung*; Carlo Maria Giulini (Italian), conducting the Philharmonia Orchestra and Chorus in the Verdi *Requiem*; Silvio Varviso (Swiss), conducting Glyndebourne's *Le Nozze de Figaro*; Luigi Nono (Italian), conducting one of his own works; and a Londoner home again, Leopold Stokowski, who has been an American citizen for many years.

International, indeed. All this was thrilling for the Prom audiences, but not more so than for the visiting conductors, each one of whom was amazed and delighted by one of the most extraordinary and fascinating audiences he had ever encountered.

But, with so much being put into the Prom programmes, some important things were being left out. An examination of the programmes now gave the diligent Prommer the opportunity not only of enthusing about the works he would be able to hear but also of having a 'damned good grouse' about those which were missing.

In the 1964 season only eight of Beethoven's nine symphonies were performed and only three of Brahms's four, the 'casualities' being the first symphony of each composer. Again, one might look at it differently and say that only one symphony of Beethoven and only one of Brahms were left out! Mr Glock explained: 'This does not mean a lack of enthusiasm for the two missing symphonies any more than "starting with a clean sheet", as we announced a few years ago, meant that we had thrown tradition overboard! We were concerned only to avoid mechanical repetition, even of the greatest successes. The chief joy in planning these forty-nine concerts is to try to renew the tradition of the Proms: to make each season as fresh as though it were the first, and as relevant.' Symphonies by Bruckner, Nielsen, and Mahler had first Prom performances.

The championing of Haydn's symphonies went on.

Two entire evenings were devoted to his music, one of them for the first Prom performance of *The Seasons*. The experiment of introducing chamber music was tried with performances of Haydn's *Emperor* Quartet, Mendelssohn's String Octet, and Stravinsky's Octet for Wind Instruments; and, in order to achieve 'more idiomatic' performances of the music of Purcell, Bach, and Handel, two chamber orchestras – the English Chamber Orchestra and the London Mozart Players – were brought in.

There was no lack of big nights and of special celebrations in this seventieth anniversary season of the Proms. Covent Garden Opera gave a complete performance of Verdi's *Otello*, linked with the four hundredth anniversary of Shakespeare's birth, and also presented the first act of Wagner's *Die Walküre*. The Royal Liverpool Philharmonic and the BBC Northern Orchestra combined in Mahler's massive Eighth Symphony ('The Symphony of a Thousand'), and there was the world première of the performing version of Mahler's uncompleted Tenth Symphony, prepared by the British musician, Deryck Cooke, from sketches left by the composer. Britten's *War Requiem* and Vaughan Williams's Sixth Symphony were performed to mark the fiftieth anniversary of the outbreak of World War I. Glyndebourne Opera gave Mozart's *Idomeneo*, and – a nice personal touch this – Dvorak's Violin Concerto was played by his young grandson, Josef Suk. Basil Cameron celebrated his eightieth birthday in a concert with the London Symphony Orchestra. Rudolf Kempe was among the distinguished foreign conductors. Pierre Monteux was to have appeared at the Proms for the first time but the great little man died in that July at the age of eighty-nine.

Television was now showing much more interest in the Proms, transmitting ten of the concerts.

Schoenberg's opera, *Moses and Aaron*, which had had a sensational success at Covent Garden, was one of the highlights of the 1965 Prom season and, again directed by Georg Solti, won great acclaim, despite the fact that the concert performance lacked the visual excitements of the 'orgy scene' which had come in for so much comment when presented at the 'Garden'! In addition to Solti, the foreign conductors in the season were Pierre Boulez, Antal Dorati, Lamberto Gardelli, Hans Werner Henze, Rudolf Kempe, Istvan Kertesz, Gennadi Rozhdestvensky, and Virgil Thompson.

Purcell's opera *The Indian Queen* was presented, and Glyndebourne Opera brought Mozart's *Le Nozza di Figaro* and Verdi's *Macbeth*. The organ was given more prominence in the programmes, the concerto on the opening night being for that instrument, and there was rather more chamber music. Sir Malcolm Sargent celebrated his seventieth birthday with a concert of works by the British composers Walton, Elgar, and Holst.

After the foreign conductors, a foreign orchestra. The first orchestra from abroad ever to appear at the Proms was the Moscow Radio Orchestra, which played in the 1966 season under its conductor Gennadi Rozhdestvensky, who had been at the Proms the previous year. Its four programmes included the first performance in western Europe of Shostakovich's *The Execution of Stepan Razin*, and it was, incidentally, the first orchestra to appear in a *planned* Sunday Prom, though there had been a Prom on a Sunday evening during the war when government requirement of the Albert Hall had necessitated a switch of evening.

There were several newcomers to the Proms among the foreign conductors – Gary Bertini, Hans Gierster, Bernard Haitink, Jascha Horenstein, Frederik Prausnitz, and Gunther Schuller; but the Scottish National Orchestra, under its musical director Alexander Gibson, was there, too. Sir Arthur Bliss, the Master of the Queen's Music, celebrated his seventy-fifth birthday by conducting a performance of his Piano Concerto.

It was a season of very big-scale events, justifying Mr Glock in his comment: 'The Proms have moved a little further away from providing a catalogue of orchestral music during the last two centuries, and a little nearer to becoming a festival, with all that implies in freedom of choice, in standards of performance, and in events of particular interest.'

Those events included the first Prom performance of the *B Minor Mass* of Bach, all six of whose *Brandenberg* Concertos were also presented; Acts 1 and 3 of *Parsifal* by Covent Garden Opera; *The Magic Flute* by Glyndebourne Opera; Berlioz' *The Fall of Troy*; Beethoven's *Missa Solemnis*; Handel's *Solomon*; Delius's *A Mass of Life*; and Elgar's *The Dream of Gerontius*.

Yet, amidst all the excitement, sturdy old Beethoven still came in for a pat on the back. Said Mr Glock: 'It may be doubted if the Proms could survive if Beethoven had not provided a backbone to the repertory which is a source of strength in any context, and which does not spoil our appetite for new, or for very old, works in almost any context.'

By the 1967 season, the Proms could safely be said to have reached full-scale festival pitch. There were two foreign orchestras – the Amsterdam Concertgebouw and the Polish Radio Symphony – and several newcomers among the conductors. There were a dozen British orchestras, twenty-four choirs, eighty-three vocal soloists, sixty-six instrumental soloists, and no less than thirty conductors.

No wonder Mr Glock was moved to say: 'During the last few years the Proms have gradually become like an international festival, and the change has taken place not as the result of any decision, but step by step, in trying to achieve each season a more striking repertoire and higher standards of performance.'

Monteverdi's four hundredth anniversary was celebrated, and, at the other end of the time-scale, there were, for instance, Penderecki's *St Luke Passion*, Stockhausen's *Gruppen* (involving three orchestras), and Messiaen's *Et expecto resurrectionem mortuorum*. Glyndebourne presented *Don Giovanni* and Covent Garden *Fidelio*; and, for the first time at the Proms, there was opera with stage-set and costumes, and there was music played in the middle of the arena.

Not for the first time at the Proms, this last innovation was a case of one thing leading to another. It had been decided to present Benjamin Britten's *The Burning Fiery Furnace* with the same setting as at the Aldeburgh Festival but, as the work would occupy only half the evening, there arose the question of how to accommodate players in the other half. The problem was solved by erecting in the middle of the arena a sort of boxing-ring, from which there emerged not the thud of fist on jaw but the strains of Schubert's Octet.

Every note of the eight weeks' season of the Proms is broadcast nowadays, more and more of the concerts are televised, and the amount of overseas broadcasting steadily increases. It is estimated that a Proms season commands something like a hundred million listeners.

But what on earth can the huge array of musical talent cost – and do the Proms pay their way?

The essential fact is that the BBC is basically a broadcasting rather than a concert-giving organisation, and there are many features about the Proms for which the BBC does not have to pay anything extra. A big slice of broadcasting time – time that would have to be filled anyway – is filled by first-class material and, despite the number of orchestras taking part, about half of the concerts are carried by the BBC's own Symphony Orchestra.

That fact is of more vital significance than most people realise. Indeed, the presence of the BBC Symphony Orchestra is the key to the operation. Mr Glock left no doubt in my mind when I put the matter to him.

'The reason why the Proms can go on is that the BBC Symphony Orchestra does half the concerts,' he said bluntly. 'It is as simple as that. If you take that into account, the Proms pay their way. If we had to "buy" twenty-five nights of symphony orchestras, we would be at least £50,000 down each year. It is the BBC Symphony Orchestra that makes the Proms possible. Every note is broadcast – about a hundred hours of first-class broadcasting – and from our point of view the Proms are a very good bargain indeed.

They have a huge audience, with about twice as many people listening to them as to other symphony concerts. From the television point of view, the start of BBC2 meant that the Proms escaped from being just "First and Last Nights". And, of course, it is marvellous for the BBC Symphony Orchestra to have the essential opportunity to appear in public regularly. But if they didn't, the Proms would stop.'

Mr Glock readily agreed that the Proms of today constitute the biggest music festival in the world. 'But', he stressed, 'it is, of course, not just a matter of size. There are two points here. First, it is flattering but true that everyone wants to be in the Proms nowadays. There is not one orchestra in the British Isles, including chamber orchestras, that does not want to be in the Proms every year, and foreign orchestras, too, are very keen. Second, when you don't rely on, say, one or perhaps two orchestras you can get a better standard. It is very hard for any orchestra to do twenty-five good concerts during the Proms. Ours has the biggest burden but, of course, we can plan ahead. I can say to our orchestral people, "Will you please try to get in so-and-so between now and the summer?" So that they are not learning things during the Proms. With the other orchestras it is a case of noting what they are planning to do and, if we would like certain works in the Proms, hoping to have that orchestra with the same conductor and soloist.

'Sir Henry Wood did marvellous things in the conditions in which he worked. He had one orchestra and sometimes as many as sixty Proms in a season. He must just have had to rehearse the passages that would have been disasters if he had not. But now we

157

have several orchestras, with works they have already rehearsed'.

The disappearance of special nights in the week for certain composers and the fact that one can look at a Prom brochure and find that some firmly established works are not there has aroused a good deal of comment in the last few years.

'Quite a number of famous works are not *always* there now', said Mr Glock. 'There might be, for instance, one Beethoven symphony not there. Of course, Mozart and Haydn are quite a different matter – they wrote such a lot! But I never say that I must get in this or that famous work. It does not mean that I don't think it should be there; it simply means you cannot get everything in. I re-do some programmes twenty times. You change one thing for some reason or other and off you go; it is fascinating, but it is endless.

'One reason why some famous symphonic pieces might not get in is that there are evenings now when we have an opera or other very large work, which means that you are losing the time that would be required for three symphonic works. But I don't think this should go too far. I keep a watch on it.

'And the question of particular "Nights". Of course there are Wagner Nights, better than before – such things as two acts of *Die Walküre*. There are half-Beethoven Nights, about three times a season. The difference is that Friday night is not Beethoven, Monday night Wagner, and so on. But I find that the more concerts that have a bit of Beethoven the better it is for the concert. I spread Beethoven round something like seventeen concerts. He is a marvellous

158

ingredient. Wherever you have an important Beethoven work, the concert has backbone.

'There are many "traditions" that are not all that old. When people say that you have broken a tradition of the Proms they forget that it was perhaps not a tradition for the first forty years. The situation changes and Henry Wood would have been the first person to change. When people say, "You have ruined Henry Wood's Proms", I reply that that would be for Henry Wood to say if he were back now. He was all in favour of music new to the Proms. That is the basis and if you lose that I think you have lost the whole thing – the adventure.

'I don't think young people come to the Proms now to learn Beethoven. They know Beethoven quite well. The long-playing record has had an enormous influence. But people used to come to the Proms to hear Beethoven for the first time. I know I did.'

Mr Glock's approach to the Proms might be said to have started with a policy of 'anti-segregation', the breaking away from the idea of placing music in particular compartments, combined with the effort to bring in more of the important contemporary works, as well as searching backwards for interesting early music that had never been heard at the Proms – a sort of spring-cleaning of the repertory.

'There were about two hundred and forty works in the season when I began', said Mr Glock. 'Now there are not more than two hundred – and of that two hundred, perhaps a hundred have not before been heard at the Proms'.

So the process of development has gone on – the introduction of a little chamber music, the bringing in of Glyndebourne and Covent Garden, the foreign conductors, followed naturally by the foreign orchestras.

Apart from the huge radio public, some 240,000 people actually *attend* the Proms each season and to Mr Glock the Prommers are the most important of all.

'That', he said, 'is why we have tried desperately hard to keep the price at five shillings which – when you realise that one shilling at the time the Proms started would mean about seven shillings now – is actually cheaper than it used to be. But this democratic element is very important. "Standards plus Democracy" might be said to be the motto.'

Audiences steadily grow, and it is now some ten years since it became necessary to introduce a ballot for the first and last nights of the season. The last night is of course the bigger attraction with – apart from season-ticket holders – some 10,700 people applying for 3250 seats and about 5300 for 1850 standing places.

During the Prom season there is vigorous activity behind the scenes by a number of backroom boys and girls whom the audience never see; but one of them does emerge into the limelight from time to time during the evening, to the enthusiastic cheering of the Prommers, most of whom probably do not know who he is. His name is Edgar Mays, the orchestral assistant who has been with the BBC for thirty-six years, the only member of the present staff who worked with Sir Henry Wood. He accepts with dignity the special cheer he gets as he raises the piano-lid before the start of a concerto. But he does not really care for what has become a sort of rite among the Prommers. 'Sir Henry would not have liked it', he says, with finality.

160

14

'WE WANT COLIN'

A T A TIME when the Proms have become international in character, Colin Davis brings an
international reputation to his role of principal
conductor of the BBC Symphony Orchestra and
consequently the central figure of the Prom seasons.

The American critic Harold C Schonberg ends a
recent book, *The Great Conductors*,[1] by naming those of
the younger brigade who are in his view candidates
for greatness. He chooses Claudio Abbado (Italy),
Colin Davis (Britain), Bernard Haitink (Holland),
Istvan Kertesz (Hungary), Lorin Maazel (United
States), Zubin Mehta (India), and Seiji Ozawa
(Japan).

Just embarked upon his forties, Colin Davis com-
bines richly varied experience with youthful vigour
and enthusiasm – that eager, boyish skip as he jumps
on to the podium becomes increasingly familiar to
the Prom audience.

One gets the impression that, at this stage in his
life, Colin Davis is a completely integrated person, a
man who has got to know *himself* – an important stage
in the development of an artist. Soft of voice, he is
refreshingly fluent of speech, with a wide vocabulary

---

[1] *The Great Conductors*, Harold C Schonberg, Victor Gollancz Ltd.

and a gift for choosing the apt word for the expression of his precise feelings. One senses clarity of mind behind all he says. (If, by the way, he indulges in a snatch of song in order to convey the line of a particular phrase during rehearsal, his voice is a pleasing light baritone, in contrast to the usual 'conductor's voice'.) In his gestures during performance he is less flamboyant than he was in his earlier days, all part of maturing as an artist and of knowing that the only gestures that matter are those which have specific purpose.

Because of the mark he has made in presenting the music of certain composers – Mozart, Berlioz, and Stravinsky, for instance – it is easy for one to be misled into the idea that Colin Davis is a 'specialist' conductor. His experience belies the suggestion. In his days as assistant conductor of the BBC Scottish Orchestra, he had the chance of getting to grips with the symphonic repertoire, and at Sadler's Wells, where he was musical director, his activities included conducting new productions of such a varied assembly of operas as Wagner's *Tannhäuser*, Stravinsky's *Oedipus Rex* and *The Rake's Progress*, Puccini's *Tosca*, Verdi's *La Traviata*, Janacek's *The Cunning Little Vixen*, Richard Strauss's *Ariadne on Naxos*, Bizet's *Carmen*, Mozart's *Idomeneo*, *The Magic Flute* and *Cosi Fan Tutte*, Kurt Weill's *The Rise and Fall of the City of Mahagonny*, Weber's *Der Freischütz*, and the immensely successful world première of Richard Rodney Bennett's *The Mines of Sulphur*, as well as revivals of, for instance, Beethoven's *Fidelio*, Mozart's *Don Giovanni*, and Wagner's *The Flying Dutchman*.

Indeed, it was Wagner who first thrilled him as a child, the son of a bank clerk in Weybridge.

162

'I grew up with gramophone records – bits of the "Ring" and so on – and one of my boyhood vices at about the age of nine was to hope that everybody would go for a walk so that I could play the last scene of *Siegfried* yet again', he will tell you. 'I got to know the standard symphonic classics by listening to the BBC Symphony Orchestra, conducted by Sir Adrian Boult, who presented them in an utterly uncomplicated and faithful way. We should all be grateful to him for that. He did not interfere or mess them about. You really heard, say, Beethoven's Seventh Symphony. There it was'.

Colin Davis's instrument was the clarinet, not by choice but because it was more or less thrust upon him.

'It was when I went to Christ's Hospital and was asked if I would like to play an instrument in the military band. Both my brothers had been there and had not played anything – and so they tried it on me. I was given a clarinet. I don't quite know why – I suppose it was the only thing available in the military band at the time. But it was then that music just enveloped me completely and became the chief way of looking at life.

'When the time came for me to say what I wanted to be and I said "a musician", it was a case of "Tut, tut! My dear boy, why not something nice and sensible, like a doctor? Musicians don't earn any money and it is a very terrible and insecure life". Most of what they said was perfectly true but I had not the ears to hear and so another musician was launched on the profession.'

On a clarinet scholarship to the Royal College of Music, he studied with the late Frederick Thurston ('a marvellous man – a very, very musical person'), though from his early days he had secretly cherished the ambition to be a conductor and had spent most of his pocket money on buying miniature orchestral scores. While at the College he tried to get into the conducting class but failed, one of the reasons being that at that time he was not an adequate pianist, a handicap which he proceeded to remove by practising hard.

After his National Service in the Household Cavalry as a musician, the urge to be a conductor was stronger than ever; but it is one thing to want to be a conductor and quite a different thing to be able to find an orchestra to conduct. The chance came with the Kalmar Orchestra. Young Colin Davis joined as an instrumentalist and one day asked if he might 'have a go' as conductor. He did, and thus he had made a start on the job which he felt he must do.

Apart from conducting the Kalmar Orchestra, he had the opportunity of conducting Mozart operas with a group in Oxford and also of working with the Chelsea Opera Group. All this was experience, intensified when he was appointed assistant conductor of the BBC Scottish Orchestra in 1957, with the chance of conducting the Scottish National Orchestra in a number of concerts. His reputation gradually grew but, as often happens in the career of an artist, dramatic events suddenly thrust him into the limelight and he became one of the most talked-of figures in the musical life of this country. No less a person than Otto Klemperer fell ill when he was to conduct a concert performance of *Don Giovanni* at the Royal Festival Hall, and Colin Davis stepped in with such success that when, soon afterwards, Sir Thomas Beecham withdrew from performances of *Don Giovanni* at Glyndebourne, he was at once chosen to deputise.

The demand for his services took a sharp rise and he was invited to conduct many of the leading orchestras before and during his six years' stay at Sadler's Wells, where he became musical director, increasing his experience not only on the musical side but also in the detailed work of administration. His many fine recordings have steadily advanced his international reputation and his personal visits abroad have embraced Canada and the United States (his American début was made with the Minneapolis Symphony Orchestra in 1961) as well as many European centres, where his activities have included conducting the Berlin Philharmonic Orchestra and appearing with the London Symphony Orchestra at the Vienna Festival. He has won much acclaim at the Edinburgh Festival and, in London, one of his most spectacular successes was his thrilling performance of Berlioz' *Grande Messe des Morts* in St Paul's Cathedral. British composers have had their share of Davis's attention: Michael Tippett, for instance, and, though he was not one of his earliest loves, Elgar.

Colin Davis made a tremendous impact on the Prom audience when he conducted Stravinsky's *Oedipus Rex*, following its success at Sadler's Wells, and the Prommers took him to their hearts when he carried out with dignity the unenviable task of conducting the first and last nights during the illness of Sir Malcolm Sargent in 1967. He on his part is a man who can appreciate the great merit of the Prom audience.

'Though you have your back to the audience when you are conducting, you can sense what sort of an audience it is', he has told me. 'Silence is the thing that tells you most – dead silence. It does not tell you whether or not they are liking it, but it does tell you that they are listening to what you are playing and that their attention is held.'

One thing is certain. There is no possibility of Colin Davis's being a second edition or carbon copy of any of his distinguished predecessors.

'I think heroes can be very dangerous', he says. 'To say that is not to be arrogant. Each man's approach and style are entirely his and the problem is to find one's own. Obviously, if other people have good ideas, one makes use of them but one really begins to learn when one gives up any feelings of certainty that one is right. There may be a thousand ways of being right and they can all work if you really feel that they belong to you.'

To the Proms, Colin Davis brings an individual talent and a positive personality. One may be sure that that bronze head of Sir Henry Wood, looking out from behind the orchestra, will smile upon him.

BROWSERIE

THE PROMS ARE, from one point of view, rather like those Old School dinners, at which the chairman says, 'I should like to take wine with those who were at the school between the years so-and-so and so-and-so'. And those who stand up to represent the earlier years are not necessarily all that old in themselves, the elementary truth being that they were very young when they were at school.

So it is with the Proms. They have always encouraged young artists of distinction, many of whom went on to carve out notable careers for themselves.

The year 1901, for instance, seems a very long time ago but it has to be remembered that Wilhelm Backhaus, who then made his Prom début, was seventeen at the time – and is still making gramophone records of Beethoven's piano music today. Mark Hambourg in the same year was a little older – twenty-two. Myra Hess (later Dame Myra) made her Prom début in 1908 at eighteen.

Solomon, one of the greatest pianists this country has produced, was only twelve when he made his début in 1914 – 'this really wonderful boy', as Sir Henry Wood called him. The Cockney boy, an enormous favourite with Prom audiences, went on from triumph to triumph until he was grievously stricken by the loss of the use of his hands.

Much later in the story of the Proms was the début (1931) of another fine British pianist, Cyril Smith,

167

who also suffered grave adversity. While touring in Russia, he lost the use of his left hand; but, instead of giving up in despair, he proceeded, with his wife Phyllis Sellick, to re-learn their two-piano repertoire for three hands instead of four – and several distinguished composers wrote works specially for them.

It was typical of the spirit of Mr Smith that, when I spoke to him at that time, his immediate reaction was: 'Oh, after all, I am so much luckier than poor Solomon'.

And Leon Goossens, one of the greatest of all oboe players. He was a member of the Queen's Hall Orchestra and was eighteen when he made his solo début at a Prom. Late in life, he was involved in a car accident, seriously injuring his precious mouth but, undaunted, he went on to develop an entirely new technique to meet the changed circumstances.

The names in the following pages are intended for the Prommer to indulge in a little 'browsing', in the hope that different names may ring bells in the minds of different people.

You will find, for instance, the names of two great British singers – (Dame) Maggie Teyte and (Dame) Eva Turner – both of whom broke down the barriers against British artists abroad, Dame Maggie, famed Mélisande in Debussy's opera of that name, being acclaimed by the French, and Dame Eva, one of the greatest of Turandots, winning fame in Italy.

And the names, of course, evoke stories of some of this great array of artists.

Benno Moiseiwitsch, for instance, was a close friend of his fellow-pianist Mark Hambourg, and was therefore privileged to joke at his expense. On one occasion

Mark – who was known as a somewhat 'thunderous' player – was to have played at a Savage Club dinner but found himself committed to give a concert in Glasgow. Benno at once agreed to deputise.

On arrival at the Savage, Benno said, 'I thought you told me that Mark was playing in Glasgow?' – 'Yes, that's so' – 'I don't believe it. I can't hear him'.

Parry Jones, a musician of the highest intelligence, who sang an extraordinary range of tenor roles in opera, had an unlimited flow of stories. One of them was concerned with the time when he was a young lad up from Wales, studying music in London. Sometimes he would miss a lesson in order to pick up half-a-guinea singing at a concert. 'Now, look here, Jones', his professor told him one day, 'if you go on missing lessons like this, you'll finish up as a critic'. Parry would tell that one with great zest to his friends the critics, and, of course, one had to make an innocent pretence of not having heard it before.

Walter Widdop, famed Yorkshire-born Wagnerian tenor, had a pet story about an occasion when he had been singing in *Messiah* in a north-country town. On the following morning, he was waiting for the train to take him back to London when a stranger approached him and asked: 'Th'art Walter Widdop, aren't thee?' 'That's right', said Walter, rather pleased at being recognised. 'I thought so', said the man. 'I don't blame thee so much. I blame t'so-and-so's that sent thee'.

Some of those who appeared in early Proms achieved greater celebrity later in other capacities than those in which they were first heard. (Sir) Donald Francis

Tovey and (Sir) Walford Davies both appeared as pianists but became much better known as musicologists and teachers, Sir Walford becoming a star talker on music in the pre-war days of radio. Some others who were at the Proms as pianists are thought of to-day principally as composers: Percy Grainger, Francis Poulenc, and Arthur Benjamin, who wrote several operas (Isn't *A Tale of Two Cities* worth reviving?) and hit the financial jackpot with his jolly *Jamaican Rumba*.

One artist actually achieved the seemingly impossible by making *two* Prom débuts. Soprano Dora Labette made her Prom début in 1917 and became a very well-known concert artist. Some time later, Sir Thomas Beecham, who was then directing opera at Covent Garden, announced the first appearance in this country of an outstanding Italian soprano, Lisa Perli. Sir Thomas forbade interviews with her and made a great mystery of the whole affair. In due course, Miss Perli sang Mimi in *La Bohème* at the Garden, and was promptly recognised as Dora Labette. Though responsible for the hoax, Sir Thomas blandly protested his innocence. And Lisa Perli duly made her début at the Proms.

The lists of 'novelties' on the following pages are selective rather than exhaustive, the works being included either because they are still known today or because the composers are remembered, perhaps by other works, if not by those named here. Where no other indication is given, the performance was a world première. (E) indicates a first performance in England, (L) a first London performance, and (C) a first concert performance.

1895

Kirkby Lunn and Sims Reeves were among the soloists in the first season.

Percy Pitt, composer of one of the novelties, had many works performed in subsequent seasons, became official organist and accompanist, and, in due course, musical director of the BBC

The twenty-three novelties were:

Andersen	*Fantasia on the Dutch National Anthem* (Flute solo)	(E)
Bunning	*The Shepherd's Call*	(L)
Chopin, orch Vicars	*Nocturne in F Minor*	
Clutsam	*Carnival Scenes*	
D'Erlanger	*Second Suite Symphonique*	
Halvorsen	*Boyard's March*	(E)
Kistler	Chromatic Concert Valses from the opera *Eulenspiegel*	(L)
	March, *Festklange*	(E)
Lucas	Minuet from *Anne Hathaway*	
Mackenzie	*Eugene Aram* (Recitation with music)	(L)
Massenet	Meditation from *Thaïs*	(L)
	Overture, *Phèdre*	(L)
Moszkowski	Introduction and ballet music, *Boabdil*	(L)
Pitt, Percy	*Suite in Four Movements*	
Rimsky-Korsakov	Overture, *La Nuit de Mai*	(L)
Scharwenka	Prelude to opera, *Mataswinther*	(E)
Schloesser, orch Vicars	Grand March, *Les Enfants de la Garde*	
Schubert, orch Vicars	*Military March*	
Stanford	*Dance Suite*	
Strauss, Richard	Prelude to Act 1, *Guntram*	(E)
Svendsen	*Andante Funèbre*	(E)
Tchaikovsky	*Marche Solenelle*	(E)
Vicars	Prelude, *Rosalind*	

1896

Prom débuts included those of Ada Crossley, Ben Davies and Charles Santley.

The twenty-four novelties included:

Chabrier	*Marche Joyeuse*	(E)
	Slavonic Dance from *Le Roi malgré lui*	(E)
Chaminade	Suite, *Callirhoë*	(L)
Glazounov	*Scènes de Ballet*	(E)
Grieg	*Two Norwegian Melodies* for String Orchestra	(E)
Kistler	*Festmarsch*	(E)
Massenet	Overture, *Le Cid*	(E)
	Rhapsodie Mauresque and *Marche du Cid*	(E)
Moszkowski	Ballet suite, *Laurin*	(E)
Rimsky-Korsakov	*Capriccio Espagnol*	(E)
	Scheherazade	(E)
Rubinstein, Anton	*Valse Caprice* in E Flat	(L)
Sarasate	*Zigeunerweisen*	(L)
Tchaikovsky	Suite, *Casse-Noisette*	(E)

1897

'Cellist W H Squire made his solo début.

The ten novelties included:

Cui	*Suite-Miniature*	(E)
Tchaikovsky	Suite No 4, *Mozartiana*	(E)

1898

The twenty-four novelties included:

Coleridge-Taylor	*Four Characteristic Waltzes*	(L)
Elgar	*Three Bavarian Dances*	(L)
German	Bourrée and Gigue, *Much Ado About Nothing*	(C)
Liszt	*Hungarian Rhapsody* No 6	(L)

Massenet	Suite, *Scènes Hongroises*	(L)
Rubinstein, orch D'Indy	*Melody in F*	
Saint-Saëns	Fantasia, *Samson and Delilah*	
Strauss, Richard	*Festmarsch*	(E)
Tchaikovsky	Entr'acte and Airs de Ballet from *The Voivode*	(E)
	Symphony in four tableaux after Byron's 'Manfred'	(E)
	Fantasy, *The Tempest*	(L)
	Polonaise, *Eugene Onegin*	(C)

1899

Prom débuts included that of Hayden Coffin.
The thirty-five novelties included :

Balakirev	*Overture on Three Russian Themes*	(E)
Cui	*Premier Scherzo*	(E)
Dittersdorf	Symphony, *The Transformaton of Acteon into a Stag*	(E)
Dvorak	Symphonic poem, *Die Waldtaube*	(L)
	Symphonic poem, *Heldenlied*	(L)
Goldmark	Introduction to Act 2, *Der Kriegsgefangene*	(E)
Haydn, Michael	*Symphony in C Major*	(E)
D'Indy	*Chanson et Danses*	(E)
Ippolitoff-Ivanoff	*Suite for Orchestra*	(E)
Liadov	Valse Badinage, *A Musical Snuff-Box*	(E)
Massenet	'*Le Sommeil de Cendrillon*' and '*Menuet*' from *Cendrillon*	(E)
	Ballet music, *Hérodiade*	(L)
Moszkowski	*Polish Folk Dances*	(E)
Saint-Saëns	Prelude and Cortège, *Déjanire*	(E)
Tchaikovsky	Suite for Orchestra No 2, *Caractéristique*	(E)
	Overture, *Les Caprices d'Oxane*	(E)

173

	Symphony No 3 in D	(E)
	Danse Cosaque from opera	(E)
	Mazeppa	
	Chant sans Paroles, Op 2 No 3	(E)

1900

Prom débuts included those of Jessie Goldsack and Adela Verne.

The nineteen novelties included:

Beethoven	*Duet in G for Two Flutes*	(E)
German	Three Dances from *Nell Gwynn*	(C)
Glazounov	Ballet music, *Ruses d'Amour*	(E)
Holbrooke	*Variations on 'Three Blind Mice'*	
Lalo	Suite No 2, *Namouna*	(E)
Rachmaninoff	*Piano Concerto No 1*	(E)
Rimsky-Korsakov	Symphony No 2, *Antar*	(E)
Strauss, Richard	*Serenade in E Flat* for wind	(E)
	instruments	(E)
Tchaikovsky	*Piano Concerto No 2*	(E)

1901

Prom débuts included those of Wilhelm Backhaus, John Coates, Harry Dearth, Herbert Fryer, Mark Hambourg and Edna Thornton.

The thirty-one novelties included:

Alfven	*Symphony No 2*	(E)
Balakirev	*Symphony in C*	(E)
Elgar	*Chanson de Nuit* and *Chanson de*	(L)
	Matin	
	Elevation in B Flat, *Sursum Corda*	(L)
	Pomp and Circumstance Marches,	(L)
	Nos 1 and 2	
Glazounov	'Cello solo, *Chant de Ménestrel*	(E)
	Ballet, *The Seasons*	(E)
	Ouverture Solennelle	(E)
Macdowell	*Indian Suite*	(E)

174

Sibelius	Suite, *King Christian II*	(E)
Tchaikovsky	Suite, *Swan Lake*	(E)
	Schäferspiel from *Pique Dame*	(E)
Wagner, Seigfried	Introduction to Act 3 and 'Valse at the Fair' from *Herzog Wildfang*	(E)
Weingartner	*Symphony No 2*	(E)

1902

Prom débuts included those of Muriel Foster, Katherine Goodson, Agnes Nicholls and Robert Radford.

The twenty novelties included:

Fauré	Suite, *Pelléas et Mélisande*	(C)
Franck	*Symphonic Variations*, for piano and orchestra	(E)
Holbrooke	Symphonic poem, *The Skeleton in Armour*	(L)
D'Indy	Trilogy, *Wallenstein*	(E)
Järnefeldt	Symphonic poem, *Korsholm*	(E)
Sinding	*Violin Concerto No 1*	(L)
Smyth, Ethel	Dances from *Der Wald*	(C)
Tchaikovsky	*Symphony No 1*	(L)
	Symphony No 2	(L)
	Piano Concerto No 3	(L)
	March, Entr'acte and Overture, *Hamlet*	(L)

1903

Prom débuts included those of Frederic Austin, Fanny Davies, Gervase Elwes, Josef Holbrooke, Frank Merrick, Lionel Tertis and Mathilde Verne.

The thirty-three novelties included:

Arensky	*Piano Concerto*	(E)
Bantock	Suite, *Russian Scenes*	(L)
Boughton	Symphonic poem, *Into the Everlasting*	

175

Bowen, York	Symphonic poem, *The Lament of Tasso*	
Handel	*Concerto in F*, for two wind orchestras and strings	(E)
D'Indy	Entr'acte, *L'Estranger*	(E)
Mahler	*Symphony No 1*	(E)
Raff	*'Cello Concerto*	(L)
Rimsky-Korsakov	'Night on Mount Triglav', from *Mlada*	(E)
Scott, Cyril	*Symphony No 1*	
Sibelius	*Symphony No 1*	(E)
Strauss, Richard	Song, '*Das Thal*'	(E)
	Symphonic fantasia, *Aus Italien*	(E)
Suk	Suite, *A Fairy Tale*	(E)
Wagner	Scena and Aria from *Die Feen*	(E)
Wolf-Ferrari	*Chamber Symphony in B Flat*	(E)

1904

Prom débuts included those of York Bowen, Julian Clifford, Peter Dawson, Percy Grainger, Egon Petri and Donald Francis Tovey.

The thirty-two novelties included :

Debussy	Prelude, *L'Après-midi d'un faune*	(E)
Goldmark	Overture, *In Italien*	(E)
Handel	Cantata, *Dank sei Dir*, for organ, harp and strings	(E)
	Concerto Grosso No 12, for two pianos and strings	(L)
Sinding	*Piano Concerto in D Flat*	(E)
Tchaikovsky	Intermezzo, 'The Battle of Poltava' from *Mazeppa*	(E)
	Air, 'One moment, pray' from *Pique Dame*	(L)
	Air, 'Who can be compared', from *Iolanta*	(E)
Weber	*Theme and Variations*, for corno di bassetto and orchestra	

1905

Prom débuts included that of Irene Scharrer.
The twenty-one novelties included:

Bruch	*Suite on Russian Folk Tunes*	(E)
Harty	*Symphony in D Minor ('Irish')*	(E)
Liszt	*Hungarian Storm March*	(L)
Mahler	*Symphony No 4*	(L)
Purcell	*Three Pieces for Strings*	(L)
Schubert	Overture, *Des Teufels Lustschloss*	(L)
Sibelius	Legend, *The Swan of Tuonela*	(L)
Strauss, Richard	*Symphony in F Minor*	(L)
Tchaikovsky	Closing scene, *Eugene Onegin*	(C)
	Three pieces for violin and orchestra	(E)
	Introduction and dances from *The Opritchnik*	(E)
	Symphonic ballade, *The Voivode*	

1906

Prom débuts included that of Arthur Catterall.
The twenty-eight novelties included:

Arensky	*Variations on a Theme by Tchaikovsky*	(E)
Borodin	Finale from *Mlada*	(L)
Busoni	Suite from Gozzi's *Turandot*	(E)
	Eine Lustspiel-Ouvertüre	(E)
Glière	*Symphony in E Flat*	(E)
Lalo	*Violin Concerto in G Minor on Russian Themes*	(L)
Liadov	*Eight Russian Folk Songs*, for Orchestra	(E)
	Baba-Yaga	(E)
Moussorgsky	*Gopak*	(E)
Sibelius	Tone poem, *En Saga*	(L)
	Symphonic poem, *Finlandia*	(L)
	Suite, *Karelia*	
Wagner	Isolde's narrative, *Tristan und Isolde*	(C)

| Vaughan Williams | *Norfolk Rhapsody No 1* | |

1907

The thirty-three novelties included :

Bach	Cantata, *Amore traditore*, for bass and orchestra	(E)
Bantock	Orchestral poem, *Lalla Rookh*	
Brian, Havergal	*New English Suite*	(L)
	Overture, *For Valour*	
Bridge	Symphonic poem, *Isabella*	
Delius	*Piano Concerto in C Minor*	(E)
Elgar	March, *Pomp and Circumstance*, No 4	
Harty, Hamilton	*Comedy Overture*	(L)
	Aria, *Ode to a Nightingale*	
D'Indy	*Symphonie Montagnarde*, for piano and orchestra	(E)
Mozart	*Concerto in F*, for three pianos and orchestra	(E)
Quilter	*Serenade for small orchestra*	
Ravel	*Introduction and Allegro*, for harp and orchestra	(E)
Reger	*Serenade in G* for orchestra	(E)
Sibelius	*Dance Intermezzo No 2*	(E)
	Violin Concerto	
	Overture, *Karelia*	(E)

1908

Prom débuts included those of Clara Butterworth and Myra Hess.

The seven novelties included :

Debussy	Aria, *Le Jet d'Eau*	(E)
Duparc	Aria, *Phidylé*	(E)
Gardiner, Balfour	*Symphony in E Flat*	

1909

Prom débuts included those of Ethel Hook and Szigeti.
  The thirty-six novelties included:

Bach	*Suite in G*, for strings	
Berlioz	Aria, *The Danish Huntsman*	(L)
Coates	*Four New Shakespearean Songs*, with orchestra	(L)
Davies, Walford	*Solemn Melody*, for organ and strings	(C)
Dvorak	*Humoreske*	
Haydn	*Violin Concerto No 1*	(E)
	Violin Concerto No 2	(E)
Mahler	*Adagietto*, for strings and harp	(E)
Moussorgsky	*A Song of the Flea*	(E)
	Humorous scene, *The Peep Show*	(E)
	Scena, *King Saul*	
Paderewski	*Piano Concerto in A Minor*	(L)
Ravel	*Rapsodie Espagnole*	(E)
Reger	*Variations and Fugue upon a Merry Theme*	(E)
	Symphonic Prologue to a Tragedy	(E)
Schumann	*Concertstück*, for four horns and orchestra	(E)
Sibelius	Suite for orchestra, *Swan-White*	(E)
Stanford, arr	*Two Songs*, with Orchestra	
Henry J Wood	*Fantasia on Welsh Melodies*	
	Fantasia on Scottish Melodies	

1910

The sixteen novelties included:

| Bax | Tone poem, *In the Faery Hills* |
| Vaughan Williams | *Fantasia on English Folk Song* |

179

1911

Prom débuts included those of George Baker, Margaret Balfour, Marjorie Hayward, Frank Mullings, Dorothy Silk, and Carrie Tubb.

The seventeen novelties included:

Alfven	Swedish Rhapsody, *Midsommarvaka*	(E)
Bach–Mahler	*Suite for orchestra*	(E)
Debussy	Suite, *Children's Corner*	(E)
Enesco	*Roumanian Rhapsody* No 1	(E)
	Suite for orchestra	(E)
Gardiner, Balfour	*Shepherd Fennel's Dance*	(E)
Ravel	*Pavane pour une infante défunte*	(L)

1912

Prom débuts included that of Daisy Kennedy.

The twenty-four novelties included:

Bach	*Piano Concerto* No 2 in E Major	(E)
Bridge	Suite, *The Sea*	
Elgar	*Four Songs*, with orchestra	
	Suite, *The Crown of India*	(L)
Enesco	*Roumanian Rhapsody* No 2	(E)
Glazounov	Introduction and Dance, *Salome*	(E)
Quilter	*Where the Rainbow Ends*, Suite	
Schoenberg	*Five Orchestral Pieces*	(E)
Coleridge-Taylor	*Violin Concerto in G Minor*	
Wolf-Ferrari	Introduction to Acts 2 and 3, *The Jewels of the Madonna*	(C)

1913

Prom débuts included those of Max Derewski and Phyllis Lett.

The thirty novelties included:

Bax	Two orchestral sketches, *Pensive Twilight* and *The Dance of Wild Irravel*

Brian, Havergal	Comedy overture, *Dr Merryheart*	
Coates, Eric	*Idyll*, for Orchestra	
Debussy	*Iberia, Images pour Orchestre* No 2	(E)
Dohnányi	*Suite for orchestra* in F Sharp Minor	(E)
Fauré	*Ballade*, for piano and orchestra	(E)
Glazounov	*Piano concerto in F Minor*	(E)
Goossens	*Variations on an Old Chinese Air*	
Grainger	*Shepherd's Hey*	
Rachmaninov, orch H J Wood	*Prelude in C Sharp Minor*	
Ravel	*Valses Nobles et Sentimentales*	(E)
Scott, Cyril	*Two Poems*, for orchestra	
Stravinsky	Suite, *The Firebird*	(E)
Vaughan Williams	Suite, *The Wasps*	

1914

Prom débuts included those of Norman Allin, Walford Davies, Darrell Fancourt, Joseph Farrington, Leon Goossens, Plunket Greene, Walter Hyde, Herbert Langley, Benno Moiseiwitsch, Albert Sammons and Solomon.

The twenty-two novelties included:

Bartok	*Suite* No 1, for orchestra	(E)
Boughton	*Love and Night*, for orchestra	
Bridge	*Dance Rhapsody*, for orchestra	
Davies, Walford	*Conversations* for piano and orchestra	
Elgar	Adagio *Sospiri*	
Franck	Symphonic poem, *Les Eolides*	(E)
Gardiner, Balfour	*In May-time*	
Goossens, Eugene	Symphonic poem, *Perseus*	
Holbrooke	*Imperial March*	
Schmitt, Florent	*Suite for Orchestra*	(E)
Stravinsky	*Scherzo Fantastique* for orchestra	(E)
Coleridge-Taylor	Rhapsody for Orchestra, *From the Prairie*	(L)

1915

Prom débuts included those of Elsie Cochrane and William Murdoch.

The fourteen novelties included:

Bach	*Concerto in C Minor*, for two violins and strings	
Bridge, Frank	*Lament*, for string orchestra	
Coates, Eric	Song Cycle, *The Mill o' Dreams*	
Debussy	*Le Martyre de Saint Sébastien* (*Fragments Symphoniques*)	(E)
	First Rhapsody, for clarinet and orchestra	(E)
Mascagni	Introduction, 'Iris' (*The Sun*)	(E)

1916

Prom débuts included those of Rosina Buckman, Arthur de Greef, Melsa, Elsa Stralia and Ruth Vincent.

The nineteen novelties included:

Glazounov	*Paraphrase on the Hymns of the Allied Nations*	(E)
	Song of the Hauliers on the Volga	
Grainger	Clog Dance, *Handel in the Strand*	
Handel	*Concerto No 6 in G Minor*, for two violins, 'cello, organ, and strings	
Macdowell	*Poéme Erotique* and *Scotch Poem*	(E)
Moussorgsky	*Intermezzo in B Minor*, for orchestra	(E)
	Persian Dance from *Khovanstchina*	(E)
Prokofiev	*Humorous Scherzo*, for four bassoons	
Rimsky-Korsakov	Suite for orchestra, *Pan Voyevoda*	(E)
Scriabin	*Scherzo for orchestra*	(E)

1917

Prom débuts included those of Walter Glynne and Dora Labette.

The fifteen novelties included:

Albeniz	Nivian's Dance from opera *Merlin*	
Butterworth	Rhapsody, *A Shropshire Lad*	(L)
Granados	*Five Spanish Dances*	(E)
Ireland	Prelude, *The Forgotten Rite*	
Liadov	Legend for orchestra, *Kikimora*	(E)
Palmgren	*Finnish Lullaby*, for strings	(L)

1918

Prom débuts included that of Vladimir Rosing.

The fourteen novelties included:

Bach	*Violin Concerto in G Minor*	(E)
Carpenter, John Alden	Suite, *Adventures in a Perambulator*	(E)
Duparc	*Aux Etoiles*	(E)
Malipiero, F.	*Impressioni dal Vero*, for orchestra	(E)

1919

Prom débuts included those of Harold Samuel and Megan Thomas.

The twenty-eight novelties included:

Albeniz	'Cordoba' from *Chants d'Espagne*	
Bax	*Scherzo for orchestra*	
Berners	*Fastasie Espagnole*	
Butterworth	Idyll for orchestra, *The Banks of Green Willow*	
Casella	Suite, *Le Couvent sur l'Eau*	(E)
Coates	Suite, *Summer Days*	(L)
Debussy	*La Cathédrale Engloutie*, for orchestra	

183

Grainger	Children's March, *Over the Hills and Far Away*	(L)
Moussorgsky	*Songs of the Nursery*, for voice, and orchestra	(E)
Quilter	*Children's Overture*	
Tcherepnin	*Quartet for four horns*	
Widor	*Sinfonia Sacra*, for organ and orchestra	(E)
	Symphony in F Minor, for organ and orchestra	(E)

1920

Prom débuts included those of Harriet Cohen, Harold Craxton, Astra Desmond, Maurice d'Oisly, Edith Furmedge, Beatrice Harrison, Frederic Lamond, and Lauritz Melchior.

The sixteen novelties included:

Bax	*Symphonic Variations in E*, for piano and orchestra	
Bowen, York	*Violin Concerto in E Minor*	
Fauré	*Fantaisie*, for piano and orchestra	(E)
	Suite for orchestra, *Masques et Bergamasques*	(L)
Goossens, Eugene	Symphonic poem, *The Eternal Rhythm*	
Prokofiev	*Piano Concerto No 1 in D Flat*	(E)

1921

Prom débuts included those of Brailowsky, Muriel Brunskill, Malcolm McEachern (later 'Jetsam' of 'Flotsam and Jetsam' with B C Hilliam), Isolde Menges, Leff Pouishnoff, and Harold Williams.

The twenty novelties included:

| Bartok | *Rhapsody for piano and orchestra* | (E) |
| Bliss | *Mêlée Fantasque*, for orchestra | |

Butterworth	*Two English Idylls*	
Dieren, Van	*Les Propous des Beuveurs* – '*Introit*'	
Howell, Dorothy	Ballet, *Koong Shee*	
Hughes, Herbert	*Parodies*, for voice and orchestra	
Jarnefelt	Suite for orchestra, *The Promised Land*	(E)
Offenbach	Serenade, *The Goldsmith of Toledo*	(E)
Sargent, Malcolm	Orchestral poem, *An Impression of a Windy Day*	(L)

1922

Prom débuts included those of Florence Austral, Jelly d'Aranyi, John T Cockerill, Tudor Davies, Topliss Green, Marie Hall, Percy Heming and Maggie Teyte.

The twenty novelties included :

Bloch, Ernest	*Schelemo*, Hebrew rhapsody for 'cello and orchestra	(E)
Holbrooke	Prelude, *Bronwen*	(L)
McEwen, J B	*A Winter Poem*	
Milhaud	*Suite Symphonique* No 2	(E)
Roussel	*Pour une fête de printemps*	(E)
Sargent, Malcolm	*Nocturne and Scherzo*	(L)

1923

Prom débuts included those of Bella (later Isobel) Baillie, Aubrey Brain, Joseph Hislop, José Iturbi, Jean Pougnet, Rae Robertson, Stiles-Allen and Frank Titterton.

The twenty novelties included :

Arensky	*Song of the Water-Nymph*	
Cassado	*Hispania*, Spanish Fantasy for piano and orchestra	(E)
Davies, Walford	*Memorial Suite in C*, for piano and orchestra	
Dohnányi	*Violin Concerto in D Minor*	(E)
Foulds	*Keltic Suite*	(L)

185

Gibbs, Armstrong	Poem for orchestra, *A Vision of Night*	
Greenbaum	*A Sea Poem*	
Holst	*Fugal Concerto*, for flute, oboe and strings	(C)
	Fugal Concerto	(C)
Howell, Dorothy	*Piano Concerto in D Minor*	
Korngold	Suite, *Much Ado About Nothing*	(E)
Mackenzie	Ballet music, *St John's Eve*	
Miaskovsky	Poem for orchestra, *Alasta*	(E)
Reger	*Piano Concerto in F Minor*	(E)
Saint-Saëns	Suite, *Le Carnaval des animaux*	(E)
Smyth, Ethel	*Four Choral Preludes*	

1924

Prom débuts included those of Ethel Bartlett, May Busby, Arthur Cox (later Arthur Carron), Clifford Curzon, Evelyn Scotney, Walter Widdop and Marie E Wilson.

There were no novelties this season.

1925

Prom débuts included those of Arthur Benjamin, Harold Darke, Keith Falkner, Walter Gieseking, Marie Goossens, Betty Humby, Parry Jones, Denise Lassimonne, Robert Naylor, Frank Phillips and Steuart Wilson.

The twenty-one novelties included:

D'Albert	Suite, *Aschenputtel*	(E)
Bartok	*Dance Suite*	(E)
Ibert	*The Ballad of Reading Gaol*, for orchestra	(E)
Pfitzner	Three Preludes, *Palestrina*	(E)
Taylor, Deems	Suite, *Through the Looking Glass*	(E)
Tcherepnin	Suite, *The Romance of a Mummy*	(E)

1926

Prom débuts included those of John Brownlee, Robert Easton and Bernard Shore.

The sixteen novelties included :

Bliss	Introduction and Allegro for full orchestra	
Boughton	Overture, *The Queen of Cornwall*	(L)
Coates	Phantasy for orchestra, *The Three Bears*	
Dohnányi	*Ruralia Hungarica*	(E)
Hanson, Howard	Symphonic poem, *Pan and the Priest*	
Hindemith	*Concerto for orchestra*	(E)
D'Indy	*La Queste de Dieu*, Symphonie Descriptive	(C)
Jacob	*Viola Concerto in C Minor*	(C)
Malipiero	*Il Molino della Morte*	(E)
Tailleferre	*Ballade*, for piano and orchestra	(E)

1927

Prom débuts included those of Maurice Cole, Noel Eadie, Arthur Fear, Victor Hely-Hutchinson, Roy Henderson, Miriam Licette, Angus Morrison, Heddle Nash, Sylvia Nelis, Dennis Noble, Stuart Robertson and Elsie Suddaby.

The nine novelties included :

Alwyn	*Five Preludes for orchestra*	
Dupré, Marcel	*Cortège et Litanie* for organ and orchestra	(E)
Hindemith	*Piano Concerto No 1*	(E)
Hely-Hutchinson	*Variations for orchestra*	(E)
Walton	Overture, *Portsmouth Point*	(L)
Wood, Thomas	*A Seaman's Overture*	(L)

1928

Prom débuts included those of Marian Anderson, Trefor Jones and Ina Souez.

187

The fourteen novelties included:

Bach–Schoenberg	Two *Choralvorspiele* for orchestra	(E)
Benjamin	*Concertino*, for piano and orchestra	
Casella	*Partita*, for piano and orchestra	(E)
Goldmark, Rubin	*A Negro Rhapsody*	(C)
Kodály	Suite, *Háry János*	(E)
Sibelius	Symphonic poem, *Tapiola*	(E)
Strauss, Richard	Parergon to the *Sinfonia Domestica*, for piano and orchestra	(E)

1929

Prom débuts included those of May Blyth, Enid Cruickshank and Olive Groves.

The nineteen novelties included:

Bax	*Three Orchestral Pieces*	
Berkeley	*Suite for orchestra*	(E)
Bliss	*Concerto for two pianos and orchestra*	(E)
Honegger	*Concertino*, for piano and orchestra	(L)
	Rugby, Mouvement Symphonique	(E)
Hely-Hutchinson	*A Carol Symphony*	(L)
Howells, Herbert	*In Green Ways*, Song-group for soprano and orchestra	(L)
Lambert	*Music for orchestra*	(C)
Miaskovsky	Symphonic poem, *Silentium*	(E)
Moeran	*Rhapsody No 2*	(L)
Tommasini	*Prelude, Fanfare and Fugue*	(E)
Walton	*Viola Concerto*	
Wilson, Stanley	*Piano Concerto*	

1930

Prom débuts included those of Norah Gruhn, Eda Kersey, Kathleen Long, Ernest Lush, Gladys Ripley and Oda Slobodskaya.

The twelve novelties were:

Bridge	Rhapsody for orchestra, *Enter Spring*	(L)

Dupré, Marcel	*Symphony for orchestra and organ*	(E)
Goossens, Eugene	*Oboe Concerto*	
Grainger, Percy	*English Dance*, for orchestra and organ	(E)
Honegger	*'Cello Concerto*	(E)
Ireland	*Piano Concerto*	
Janacek	*Wallachian Dances*, for orchestra	(E)
Kodály	*Summer Evening (Nyari Este)*	(E)
Krenek	*Potpourri for orchestra*	(L)
Maconchy, Elizabeth	Suite, *The Land*	
Smyth, Ethel	*Anacreontic Ode*, for baritone and orchestra	(C)
Villa-Lobos	*Chôros* (No 8) for full orchestra	(E)

1931

Prom débuts included those of Joan Cross, Francis Poulenc, Cyril Smith, Conchita Supervia and Emil Telmanyi.
The six novelties included:

Elgar	*Nursery Suite*	
Delius	*A Song of Summer*	
Fogg, Eric	*Bassoon Concerto in D Major*	
Webern	*Passacaglia*, for orchestra	(E)

1932

The three novelties included:

Ravel	*Piano Concerto for the left hand*	(E)

Winter Season 1932–3

The novelties were:

Hindemith	*Philharmonic Concerto*	(E)
Smyth, Ethel	*Fête galante*	(L)

189

1933

Prom débuts included those of Renee Chemet, Laelia Finneberg, Mary Jarred and Sophie Wyss.

The novelties were:

Delius	*Idyll*, for soprano, baritone and orchestra	
Gerhard	*Six Catalan Folk-songs*, for soprano and orchestra	(E)
Goossens, Eugene	*Kaleidoscope*	(E)
Honegger	*Symphonic Movement No 3*	(E)

1934

Prom débuts included that of Luella Paikin.

The twelve novelties included:

Bach–Respighi	*Prelude and Fugue in D*	
Converse, Frederick	*California*	(E)
Kodály	*Dances of Galanta*	(E)
Taylor, Deems	*Circus Day*	(E)
Toch, Ernst	*Symphony for piano and orchestra*	
Vaughan Williams	*The Running Set*	

Winter Season 1934–5

The novelty was:

Smyth, Ethel	*Entente Cordiale*

1935

Prom débuts included those of Elena Gerhardt (deputising for indisposed Conchita Supervia), Eileen Joyce and Elisabeth Schumann.

The novelties were:

Bartok	*Hungarian Peasant Songs*	(E)
Berkeley, Lennox	*Overture*	(E)

190

Bliss	*Suite from Film Music* – 1935	(C)
Bush, Alan	*Dance Overture*	(C)
Fogg, Eric	*September Night*	(C)
Howells, Herbert	*Elegy*, for strings	(L)
Jacob, Gordon	*Passacaglia on a Well-known Theme*	(L)
Larsson, Lars-Erik	*Saxophone Concerto*	(E)
Sainton, Philip	*Serenade Fantastique* for viola and orchestra	
Shostakovich	*Symphony No 1*	(L)
Stephen, David	*Coronach*	(L)
Tailleferre	*Concerto for two pianos, mixed chorus, saxophones and orchestra*	(E)

1936

Prom débuts included those of Lisa Perli and Artur Rubinstein.

The novelties were:

Bach–Casella	*Chaconne*, for full orchestra	(E)
Bantock	Comedy overture, *The Frogs*	
Dohnányi	*Minutes Symphoniques*	(E)
Greenwood, John	*Salute to Gustav Holst*	(C)
Ibert	*Concertino da Camera* for saxophone and orchestra	(E)
Ireland	*A London Overture*	
Maconchy, Elizabeth	*Piano Concerto*	(E)
Marsick, Armand	*Tableaux Grecs*	(E)
Sibelius	Ballad for mezzo-soprano and orchestra, *The Ferryman's Bride*	(E)
Vogel, Vladimir	*Ritmica Ostinata*	(E)
Whyte, Ian	*Three Scottish Dances*	(L)

1937

Prom débuts included that of Redvers Llewellyn.

The novelties were:

| Austin, Frederick | Overture, *The Sea Venturers* | (L) |

Bax	*London Pageant*	(C)
Rossini-Britten	*Soirées Musicales*	(C)
Gibbs, Armstrong	*Essex Suite* for strings	(L)
Handel	*Five Choruses from the operas*	(C)
Purcell–Herbage	Suite from *King Arthur* for strings	(L)
Ibert	*Escales*	(L)
Jacob, Gordon	*Variations on an Original Theme*	(L)
Kodály	*Ballet Music*	(E)
Malipiero	*Violin Concerto*	(E)
Rubbra	*Fantasia for violin and orchestra*	
Tailleferre	*Harp Concerto*	(E)

1938

Prom débuts included those of Webster Booth, Benjamin Britten and Moura Lympany.

The novelties were:

Bliss	Film Music, *Conquest of the Air*	(C)
Britten	*Piano Concerto*	
Jacob, Gordon	*Helen of Kirconnell*	(E)
Lambert, Constant	Suite from ballet, *Horoscope*	
Lewis, Anthony	*Overture for unaccompanied chorus*	
Milhaud	*Suite Provençale*	(E)
Poot, Marcel	*Allegro Symphonique*	(L)
Rachmaninov	Prelude to opera, *The Avaricious Knight*	(E)
Roussel	*Rapsodie Flamande*	(E)
Walton	*Façade* (Second Suite)	

1939

Prom débuts included those of Joan Hammond, Louis Kentner, Denis Matthews, and Richard Tauber. The season was curtailed because of the outbreak of war.

1940

Prom débuts included that of Ida Haendel. The season was again curtailed.

The novelties included:

Elizabeth Lutyens *Three Pieces for Orchestra*

1941

Prom débuts included that of Eda Kersey.

The novelties included:

Samuel Barber	*Symphony in One Movement*	(E)

1942

Prom débuts included those of Colin Horsley, Janet Howe, and Mary and Geraldine Peppin.

The novelties were:

Benjamin, Arthur	Rondo for orchestra, *Prelude to Holiday*	(E)
Britten	*Sinfonia da Requiem*	(E)
Bush, Alan	*Symphony in C*	
Cimarosa-Benjamin	*Oboe Concerto*	(E)
Copland, Aaron	Ballet suite, *Billy the Kid*	(E)
Demuth, Norman	*Valses Graves et Gaies*	
Dunhill, T F	*Triptych*, Three Impressions for Viola and Orchestra	
Farjeon, Harry	Symphonic Poem, *Pannychis*	
Gipps, Ruth	Symphonic Poem, *Knight in Armour*	
Harris, William H	*Heroic Prelude*	
Ireland, John	*Epic March*	
Lucas, Leighton	*Suite Française*	
Lucas, Mary Anderson	*Circus Suite*	

193   N

Maconchy, Elizabeth	*Dialogue* for Piano and Orchestra	
Moeran, E J	*Violin Concerto*	
Roley, Alec	*Three Idylls* for piano and orchestra	
Rubbra, Edmund	*Symphony No 4*	
Shostakovich	*Symphony No 7* (*Leningrad*)	(E)

1943

Prom débuts included those of Antony Hopkins, Phyllis Sellick, and Joan and Valerie Trimble.

The novelties were :

Alexandrov	*Overture on Russian Folk Tunes*	(E)
Berkeley, Lennox	*Symphony*	
Britten	*Scottish Ballad* for two pianos and orchestra	(E)
Budashkin	*Festival Overture*	(E)
Busch, William	*'Cello Concerto*	
Chavez, Carlos	*Sinfonia India*	(E)
Copland, Aaron	*A Lincoln Portrait*	(E)
Dunhill, T F	*Waltz Suite*	
Goossens, Eugene	*Symphony No 1*	(E)
Gundry, Inglis	*Heyday Freedom*	
Kabalevsky	Suite from *Colas Breugnon*	(E)
Khachaturyan	*Lezginka*	(E)
Moeran, E J	*Rhapsody*, for piano and orchestra	
Piston, Walter	*Sinfonietta*	(E)
Rowley, Alec	*Burlesque Quadrilles*	
Rubbra, Edmund	*Sinfonia Concertante* for piano and orchestra	
Schuman, William	*Symphony No 3*	(E)
Shebalin	*Overture*	(E)
Stringfield, Lamar	Symphonic Patrol *A Negro Parade*	(E)
Van Wyk, Arnold	*Saudade*, for violin and orchestra	

194

Weber	*Concertstuck*
Weisgall, Hugo	*American Comedy 1943*
Vaughan Williams	*Symphony in D*

1944

Prom débuts included that of Nina Milkina.   The season was curtailed because of flying bombs.

The novelties were:

Bantock, Granville	*Two Hebridean Sea Poems*	
Barber, Samuel	*Violin Concerto*	(E)
Goossens, Eugene	*Fantasy Concerto*, for two pianos and orchestra	(E) (E)
Phillips, Montague	*In Praise of my Country*	

1945

Prom débuts included those of Ada Alsop, Valda Aveling, Daria Bayan, Owen Brannigan, Alfredo Campoli, Nancy Evans, David Lloyd, Ginette Neveu, and Peter Pears.

The novelties were:

Britten	Four Interludes and Passacaglia, *Peter Grimes*	(CL)
Bush, Alan	*Fantasia on Russian Themes*	
Dunhill, T F	Overture, *May-Time*	
Evans, David Moule	Poem for Orchestra, *September Dusk*	
Hadley, Patrick	*Travellers*, for soprano, chorus and orchestra	(L)
Hindemith	Ballet Overture, *Cupid and Psyche*	(E)
Martinu	*Memorial to Lidice*	(E)
Noble, Tertius	*Introduction and Passacaglia*	(L)
Rawsthorne	Fantasy Overture for Orchestra, *Cortèges*	
Schoenberg	*Piano Concerto*	(E)

Schuman, William	*A Free Song*, for chorus and orchestra	(E)
Veprik	*Song of Jubilation*	(E)
Walton	Suite from *Henry V*	(C)
Whyte, Ian	*Festival March*	
Vaughan Williams	Suite, *The Story of a Flemish Farm*	(C)
	Thanksgiving for Victory	(C)

1946

Prom débuts included those of Iso Elinson, Pierre Fournier, Arthur Grumiaux, Alan Loveday, Malcuzynski, Yehudi Menuhin, Max Rostal, Victoria Sladen, and Jo Vincent.

The novelties were:

Bliss	Suite, *Adam Zero*	(C)
Bloch	*Suite Symphonique*	(E)
Britten	*Piano Concerto No 1 in D* (revised version)	(L)
Creston	*Poem*, for harp and orchestra	(E)
Hindemith	*Symphonic Metamorphoses on Themes of Weber*	(E)
Ireland	Overture, *Satyricon*	
Lucas, Leighton	*Litany*, for orchestra	(C)
Milhaud	*Deux Marches*	(E)
Prokofiev	*Symphony No 5*	(E)
Shostakovich	*Symphony No 9*	(E)
Strauss, Richard	*Oboe Concerto*	(E)
Stravinsky	*Scherzo à la Russe*	(E)
Walton	*Where Does the Uttered Music Go?* for unaccompanied chorus	(C)

1947

Prom débuts included those of Kathleen Ferrier, Zara Nelsova and Mewton Wood.

The novelties were:

| Chagrin | *Prelude and Fugue* for Orchestra | |
| Duruflé, Maurice | *Trois Danses* | (E) |

Goossens, Eugene	*Three Pictures*, for flute, strings and percussion	(E)
Haydn	*Concerto in C*, for organ	(E)
Hely-Hutchinson	*Symphony*, for small orchestra	(L)
Jacob, Gordon	*Concerto*, for bassoon, strings and percussion	
Lewis, Anthony	*Elegy and Capriccio*, for trumpet and orchestra	
Lutyens, Elizabeth	*Petite Suite*	(CL)
Novák, Viteslav	*Triptych on a Chorale Theme from St Wenceslas*	
Piston, Walter	*Symphony No 2*	(E)
Rawsthorne	*Concerto*, for oboe and strings	(L)
Rubbra, Edmund	*Festival Overture*	(L)
Schuman, William	*Piano Concerto*	(E)
Starokadomsky	*Concerto* for orchestra	(E)

1948

Prom débuts included those of Margherita Grandi, Yfrah Neaman, and Paul Tortelier.

The novelties were:

Auric, Georges	*Overture*	(E)
Berkeley, Lennox	*Piano Concerto in B Flat*	
Cooke, Arnold	*Processional Overture*	(L)
Grainger, Percy	*Danish Folk Music Suite*	(E)
Jaubert	*Suite Française*	(E)
Kabalevsky	*Piano Concerto No 2*	(E)
Milhaud	*Suite Française*	(E)
Moeran, E J	*Seranade in G* for orchestra	
Mozart	*Oboe Concerto in C*	(E)
Rawsthorne	*Violin Concerto*	(L)
Scott, Cyril	*Oboe Concerto*	
Searle, Humphrey	*Fugue* for orchestra	
Stevens, Bernard	*Fugal Overture*	
Vaughan Williams	*Partita* for double string orchestra	(C)

197

1949

Prom débuts included those of Gre Brouwenstijn, Geraint Evans, Sylvia Fisher, Julius Katchen, Richard Lewis, and Elsie Morison.

The novelties were:

Berkeley, Lennox	*Colonus' Praise*	
Bloch	*Concerto Symphonique* for piano and orchestra	(L)
Buch, Alan	*Violin Concerto*	
Goossens, Eugene	*Fantasy* for piano and orchestra	
	Sinfonietta	(L)
Honegger	*Symphony No 3*	(CE)
Jacob, Gordon	*Fantasia on the Alleluia Hymn*	(L)
Lucas, Leighton	*Chaconne in C Sharp Minor*	(C)
Rawsthorne	*Concerto* for string orchestra	(E)
Searle, Humphrey	*Overture to a Drama*	
Strauss, Richard	*Duet Concertino* for clarinet, string orchestra and harp	(L)

1950

Prom débuts included those of Robert Casadesus, Suzanne Danco, Victoria de los Angeles, Adele Leigh, Janine Micheau, Elizabeth Schwarzkopf, Amy Shuard, and Jennifer Vyvyan.

The novelties were:

Bartok	*Viola Concerto*	(L)
Bax	*Concertante* for Orchestra with Piano Solo (Left hand)	(L)
Douglas, Clive	*Warra-Wirrawaal*	(E)
Frankel, Benjamin	Overture, *May Day*	(L)
Honegger	*Prelude, Fugue and Postlude*	(E)
Jacob, Gordon	*Symphonic Suite* (Suite No 2)	(L)
Lutyens, Elizabeth	*Viola Concerto*	
Purcell–Lambert	Ballet Suite, *Comus*	(C)
Sowerby, Leo	*Organ Concerto in C*	

198

1951

Prom débuts included those of Zino Francescatti, Marko Rothmuller, and Monica Sinclair.

The novelties were:

Bloch	*Scherzo Fantasque* for piano and orchestra	(E)
Bush, Alan	Symphonic Suite, *Piers Plowman's Day*	(E)
Castelnuovo-Tedesco	*Concerto da Camera*	
Fricker, P Racine	*Symphony No 1*	(CL)
Hindemith	*Clarinet Concerto*	(E)
Jacob, Gordon	*Galop Joyeux*	(CL)
Johnstone, Maurice	A Cumbrian Rhapsody, *Tarn Hows*	(CL)
Jones, Daniel	*Five Pieces for Orchestra*	
Sainton, Philip	*Serenade Fantastique*	(L)

1952

Prom débuts included those of Larry Adler, Gina Bachauer, Sigurd Björling, Bronislav Gimpel, Peter Katin, André Navarra, Set Svanholm, Edith Vogel, Jess Walters, Joseph Weingarten, and Inia te Wiata.

There were no premières, the stress being laid this season on giving first Prom performances of interesting works which had already been heard elsewhere.

1953

Prom débuts included those of Joseph Cooper, Victoria Elliott, Amaryllis Fleming, Andor Foldes, Howell Glynne, Rowland Jones, Beryl Kimber, Arda Mandikian, Eric Parkin, Anna Pollock, Olwen Price, Livia Rev, Sir Malcolm Sargent (as pianist), Erna Schlüter, Constance Shacklock, Ludwig Suthaus, Frans Vroons, and Alexander Young.

The novelties were :

Arnold, Malcolm	*Concerto*, for piano duet and strings	(L)
Benjamin, Arthur	*Harmonica Concerto*	
Berkeley, Lennox	*Flute Concerto*	
Hamilton, Iain	*Symphony No 2*	(L)
Howells, Herbert	*A Kent Yeoman's Wooing Song*	
Jacob, Gordon	*Violin Concerto*	
Johnstone, Maurice	*The Oak and the Ash*	(L)
Jongen, Joseph	*Symphonie Concertante*, for organ and orchestra	(L)
Malipiero	*Settima Sinfonia*	(E)
Martin, Frank	*Petite Symphonie Concertante*, for harp, harpsichord, piano and strings	
Tippett	*Fantasia Concertante on a Theme of Corelli*, for strings	(L)
Walton	*Coronation Te Deum*	(CL)
Whettam, Graham	*Concertino* for oboe and strings	(C)

1954

Prom débuts included those of Pauline Brockless, Frederick Dalberg, Mattiwilda Dobbs, Ralph Downes, Sena Jurinac, Clive Lythgoe, Martha Mödl, Norma Procter, Franz Reizenstein, Margaret Ritchie, Paul Schoeffler, Joan Sutherland, Rosalyn Tureck, Ian Wallace, and Wolfgang Windgassen.

The novelties were :

Alwyn, William	*Harp Concerto*	
ApIvor, Denis	*A Mirror for Witches*	
Benjamin, Arthur	*Symphony*	(L)
Bliss	*A Song of Welcome*	
Burkhard, Paul	Overture, *The Hunting Parson*	(E)
Cannon, Philip	Symphonic Study, *Spring*	
Fulton, Norman	*Sinfonia Pastorale*	(L)

200

Gardner, John	*A Scots Overture*	
Jolivet	*Concertino*, for trumpet, strings and piano	(E)
Leighton, Kenneth	*Violin Concertino*	
Maconchy, Elizabeth	*Concertino*, for bassoon and strings	
Rachmaninov	*Symphonic Dances*	(E)

1955

Prom débuts included those of Bruce Boyce, Julian Bream, Shura Cherkassky, Szymon Goldberg, Gwyn Griffiths, Erich Gruenberg, Ilse Hollweg, Ralph Holmes, Michael Langdon, Magda Laszlo, Marion Lowe, George Malcolm, Walter Midgley, and Helen Watts.

The novelties were:

Alwyn, William	*Autumn Legend* for cor anglais and strings	(L)
Brott, Alexander	Overture, *Royal Tribute*	(E)
Cooke, Arnold	*Oboe Concerto*	(L)
Jacob, Gordon	*'Cello Concerto*	
Menotti	Overture, *Amelia Goes to the Ball*	(CE)
Panufnik	*Sinfonia Rustica*	(CE)
Prokofiev	*Symphony No 7*	(CL)
Veale, John	*Panorama*	(CL)
Walton	Duet, Act 2, *Troilus and Cressida*	(C)
Weber	*Symphony No 1 in C*	(CE)

1956

Proms débuts included those of Lamar Crowson, Jacqueline Delman, Gervase de Peyer, Carl Dolmetsch, Elizabeth Fretwell, Heather Harper, Ronald Lewis, William McAlpine, James Milligan, Tessa Robbins, Janos Starker, Erna Spoorenberg, and Nicanor Zabaleta.

The novelties were:

| Addison, John | Suite from ballet, *Carte Blanche* | (C) |

Benjamin, Arthur	*Concerto quasi una Fantasia*, for piano and orchestra	(L)
Berkeley, Lennox	Suite, *Nelson*	(C)
Bush, Alan	*Concert Suite*, for 'cello and orchestra	(CL)
Copland, Aaron	*Symphony No 3*	(CE)
Fricker, P. Racine	*Concertante* for three pianos, strings and percussion	(CL)
Greenwood, John	*Viola Concerto*	
Hamilton, Iain	*Symphonic Variations*	(L)
Hoddinott, Alun	*Concerto*, for clarinet and strings	(CL)
Kodály	*Variations on a Hungarian Folk-song* ('Peacock')	(CL)
Lucas, Leighton	*Concert Champêtre*	(CE)
Martinu	*Suite Concertante* for violin and orchestra	
Milhaud	*Harp Concerto*	(E)
Saeverud	*Siljuslatten*	(CE)
Searle, Humphrey	*Piano Concerto No 2*	(CL)
Surinach	*Sinfonietta Flamenca*	(E)
Thompson, Randall	*The Last Words of David*	(E)
	Tarantella	(E)

1957

Prom débuts included those of Stefan Askenase, Joyce Barker, Ranken Bushby, Leonard Cassini, Mimi Coertse, Cor de Groot, Kirsten Flagstad, Maureen Forrester, Scott Joynt, Ilona Kabos, Lois Marshall, James Pease, Carmen Prietto, Robert Riefling, Forbes Robinson, Allan Schiller, and Jon Vickers.

The novelties were :

Arnold, Malcolm	*Divertimento*	(L)
Bate, Stanley	*Piano Concerto No 3*	
Blacher, Boris	*Fantasy* for orchestra	(CE)
Fricker, P Racine	*Litany*, for double string orchestra	(CL)
Hamilton, Iain	Overture, *Bartholomew Fair*	(CE)

202

Henze, Hans Werner	*Ode to the West Wind*, for 'cello and orchestra	(E)
Holmboe, Vagn	*Epitaph*	(CE)
Ibert	*Bacchanal*	(C)
Jacob, Gordon	*Piano Concerto No 2*	(L)
Jones, Daniel	*Symphony No 4* (In memory of Dylan Thomas)	(CL)
Martin, Frank	Overture, *Athalie*	(E)
Martinu	*Piano Concerto No 4*	
Panufnik	*Rhapsody for Orchestra*	(C)
Petrassi, Goffredo	*Invenzione Concertata*	
Rawsthorne	Dance Suite, *Madame Chrysanthème*	
Reizenstein, Franz	Overture, *Cyrano de Bergerac*	(CL)

1958

Prom débuts included those of Harold Blackburn, April Cantelo, Charles Craig, Osian Ellis, John Hauxvell, Thomas Hemsley, Gloria Lane, Hephzibah Menuhin, Regina Resnik, Bela Siki, Josephine Veasey, David Ward, and Daniel Wayenberg.

The novelties were :

ApIvor, Denis	*Piano Concerto*	(C)
Bush, Geoffrey	*Symphony No 1*	(L)
Butterworth, Arthur	*Symphony*	(L)
Copland, Aaron	*Orchestral Variations, 1957*	(E)
Finzi, Gerald	*The Fall of the Leaf*	(L)
Hoddinott, Alun	*Harp Concerto*	(L)
Martin, Frank	*Etudes*, for string orchestra	(E)
Shostakovich	*Piano Concerto*, Op 101	(E)
Williams, Grace	*Penillion*	(CL)

1959

Prom débuts included those of Jean Allister, Anthony di Bonaventura, Kim Borg, Peter Element, Maurice Gendron,

Natalia Karp, Kerstin Meyer, John Mitchinson, John Ogdon, Hans Richter-Haaser, Rohan de Saram, Elizabeth Simon, Roger Stalman, Malcolm Williamson, and Ilse Wolf.

The novelties were:

Alwyn, William	Symphony No 4	
Arnell, Richard	Ballet Suite, Harlequin in April	(C)
Berkeley, Lennox	Symphony No 2	(L)
Bowen, York	Piano Concerto No 4	(C)
Ibert	Symphonie Concertante, for oboe and strings	(CE)
Leighton, Kenneth	Burlesque	(C)
Maconchy, Elizabeth	Concerto, for oboe, bassoon and strings	(C)
Martinu	Oboe Concerto	(CE)
Milhaud	Concerto, for percussion and small orchestra	(CL)
Seiber, Mátyás	Tre Pezzi, for 'cello and orchestra	(CL)
Rodrigo	Concerto-Serenata, for harp and orchestra	(E)
Whettham, Graham	Dance Concertante, for two pianos (three hands) and orchestra	(L)
Williamson, Malcolm	Piano Concerto	(L)

1960

Prom débuts included those of Raffaele Ariè, Janet Baker, Donald Bell, Malcolm Binns, Joan Carlyle, Sergio Varella-Cid, Marie Collier, Elise Czerfalvi, Ronald Dowd, Ingrid Haebler, Raimund Herincz, Grace Hoffman, Patricia Johnson, Annelies Kupper, Russell Oberlin, Alberto Remedios, Charles Rosen, Anna Maria Rota, Nadine Sautereau, Jeannette Sinclair, Henryk Szering, Elisabeth Söderström, Valeria Tryon, and Peter Wallfisch.

The novelties were:

Alwyn, William	Overture, Derby Day	
Berg	Altenberglieder	(CE)

Beric	*Perspectives*	(E)
Goossens, Eugene	*Phantasy Concerto*, for violin and orchestra	(C)
Hamilton, Iain	*Scottish Dances*	(CL)
Ives, Charles	*Three Places in New England*	(CE)
Musgrave, Thea	*Triptych*, for tenor and orchestra	

1961

Prom débuts included those of Paul Baumgartner, Colin Bradbury, Gerald English, Philippe Entremont, Mirella Freni, Marina de Gabarain, Victor Godfrey, Alfred Hallett, Elizabeth Harwood, Aafje Heynis, Irma Kolassi, Yvonne Lefébure, Ilva Ligabue, Gyorgy Melis, Sybil Michelow, Leonardo Monreale, Thomas Rajna, Nell Rankin, Gerda Scheyrer, Teresa Stich-Randall, Barry Tuckwell, Tamas Vasary, Kyra Vayne, and Katharina Wolpe.

The novelties were:

Gerhard, Roberto	Two songs from *The Duenna*	(C)
Goehr, Alexander	*Hecuba's Lament*	
Hamilton, Iain	*Écossaise*	(L)
Lutyens, Elizabeth	*Symphonies*, for solo piano, wind, harps and percussion	(E)
Milner, Anthony	*Divertimento*, for string orchestra	
Ravel–Goossens	*Le Gibet* ('Gaspard de la Nuit')	(E)
Williamson, Malcolm	*Organ Concerto*	

1962

Prom débuts included those of Geza Anda, Stephen Bishop, Alan Civil, Jacqueline du Pré, Peter Glossop, Reri Grist, Stefania Malagu, Simon Preston, Hermann Prey, Michel Roux, and Grace Wilkinson.

The novelties were:

Berkeley, Lennox	*Five Pieces*, for violin and orchestra

205

Brahms– Schoenberg	*Quartet in G Minor*	(CE)
Cooke, Arnold	Ballet Suite, *Jabez and the Devil*	

Davies,
    P Maxwell
	*Fantasia on an In Nomine by John
	    Taverner*	

Maw, Nicholas	*Scenes and Arias*	
Musgrave, Thea	*The Phoenix and the Turtle*	
Rawsthorne, Alan	*Medieval Diptych*, for baritone and orchestra	
Shostakovich	*Festival Overture*	(CE)
Stravinsky	*Greeting Prelude*	(L)

1963

Prom débuts included those of Walter Alberti, Elizabeth Bainbridge, Frances Bible, Heinz Blankenberg, Grayston Burgess, Carlo Cava, Hugues Cuenod, Alfred Deller, John Dobson, Dorothy Dorow, Carlos Feller, Gottlob Frick, Leyla Gencer, Nell Gotkovsky, Alasdair Graham, Maureen Guy, Gwyneth Jones, John Kentish, Soo-Bee Lee, Maureen Lehane, Lydia Marimpietri, Valerie Masterson, Edith Mathis, Birgit Nilsson, Frank Olegario, Johanna Peters, Anna Reynolds, Annon Lee Silver, and Thomas Stewart.
    The novelties included :

Berkeley, Lennox	*Four Ronsard Sonnets*, for tenor and orchestra	
Britten	*Cantata Misericordium*	(E)
Burt, Francis	*Fantasmagoria*, for orchestra	
Fricker, P Racine	*O longs désirs* : Song Cycle for soprano and orchestra	
Nono, Luigi	Cantata : *Sul ponte di Hiroshima*	(L)

1964

Prom débuts included those of Amadeus String Quartet, Vladimir Ashkenazy, Noreen Berry, John Carol Case, Peter Frankl, Don Garrard, David Hughes, Rita Hunter, Gundula Janowitz, Mindru Katz, David Kelly, Ernst

Kozub, Kenneth MacDonald, Luciano Pavarotti, Judith Pierce, Michael Roll, Mstislav Rostropovich, Joseph Rouleau, Jusef Suk, Enriqueta Tarres, Glynne Thomas, Pauline Tinsley, Anita Valkki, Elizabeth Vaughan, John Wakefield, and Claire Watson.

The novelties included:

Alwyn, William	*Concerto Grosso No 3* (Tribute to Henry Wood)
Bennett, Richard Rodney	*Aubade* (In memory of John Hollingsworth)
Brindle, Reginald Smith	*Creation Epic* (Choreographic Suite for Orchestra)
Mahler	*Symphony No 10* (Full-length performing version by Deryck Cooke)
Naylor, Bernard	Cantata: *Sing O my love*
Rainier, Priaulx	*'Cello Concerto*

1965

Prom débuts included those of Delme Bryn-Jones, Biancamaria Casoni, Margaret Curphey, Federico Davià, Anne Howells, John Lanigan, Raymond Leppard, Jeanne Loriod, Yvonne Minton, Josephine Nendick, Kostas Paskalis, Richard Popplewell, Margaret Price, Maureen Smith, Robert Tear, Gillian Weir, and Eva Zurbrügg.

The novelties included:

Hamilton, Iain	*Cantos*, for orchestra
Maconchy, Elizabeth	*Variazioni Concertanti*, for oboe, clarinet, bassoon, horn and string orchestra
Williamson, Malcolm	*Concerto Grosso*
Wood, Hugh	*Scenes from 'Comus'*

1966

Prom débuts included those of Martha Argerich, Sheila Armstrong, Daniel Barenboim, Ryland Davies, Victor de

Narké, Stafford Dean, Gregory Dempsey, Bernard Dickerson, Nicola Gebolys, Vitaly Gromadsky, Marga Höffgen, Heinz Holliger, Ann Howard, Patricia Kern, Otakar Kraus, Halina Lukomska, Anne Pashley, Nicolai Petrov, Günter Reich, Elizabeth Robson, Arlene Saunders, Natalie Shakhovskaya, John Shaw, George Shirley, Roger Smalley, Galina Solodchin, Fritz Uhl, and Uto Ughi.

The novelties included:

Boulez	*Éclat*	(CE)
Crosse, Gordon	*Ceremony*, for 'cello and orchestra	
Ives, Charles	*The Fourth of July*	(E)
	Symphony No 4	(CE)
Rubbra	Motet: *Veni, Creator Spiritus*, for mixed choir and brass	
Schuller, Gunther	*Movements*, for flute and strings	(E)
Shostakovich	*The Execution of Stepan Razin*	(Western Europe)
Varèse	*Equatorial*	(E)

1967

Prom débuts included those of Cecil Aronowitz, Claudio Arrau, Emile Belcourt, Ingrid Bjoner, Kurt Boehme, Althea Bridges, Janet Coster, Bryan Drake, Leonid Kogan, Konstanty Kulka, Evelyn Lear, Robert Massard, Paolo Montarsolo, Margaret Neville, Rafael Orozco, Victoria Postnikova, Fou Ts'ong, Joseph Ward, Wanda Wilkomirska, and Teresa Zylis-Gara.

The novelties included:

Searle, Humphrey	*Oxus*, Scena for tenor and orchestra	
Wilson, Thomas	*Touchstone*, Portrait for orchestra	

Acknowledgements

I HAVE TO thank, among others who have helped, Sir Adrian Boult, for his kindness in writing the introduction; Lady Jessie Wood for permission to use a copyright picture; Mr William Glock, Controller of Music, BBC; and Mr Barrie Hall and his BBC colleagues for allowing me access to the complete collection of Prom programmes. The quotation from Mr Ivor Newton's *At the Piano – Ivor Newton* is included by permission of Messrs Hamish Hamilton Ltd, and that from Sir Eugene Goossens' *Overture and Beginners* by permission of Messrs Methuen and Company Ltd. The extract from a leading article is reproduced by permission of *The Times*.

Books which have bearing on the subject include *Queen's Hall*, Robert Elkin (Rider 1944); *The Royal Albert Hall*, Ronald W Clark (Hamish Hamilton 1958); *My Life of Music*, Henry J Wood (Gollancz 1938); *About Conducting*, Henry J Wood (Sylvan Press 1945); *Henry J Wood*, Rosa Newmarch (John Lane 1904); *The Last Years of Henry J Wood*, Jessie Wood (Gollancz 1954); *The Proms*, Thomas Russell (Max Parrish 1949); and *The Story of the Proms*, Patricia M Young and others (BBC 1955).

For the illustrations in this book I acknowledge the assistance of the BBC, the Radio Times Hulton Picture Library, the London *Evening News* and UPI.

LESLIE AYRE

INDEX

210

213

216